THE *UNOFFICIAL* MAD MEN COOKBOOK

Inside the Kitchens, Bars, and Restaurants of *Mad Men*

Judy Gelman and Peter Zheutlin

An Imprint of BenBella Books, Inc.

Dallas, Texas

Copyright © 2011 by Judy Gelman and Peter Zheutlin

Smart Pop is an Imprint of BenBella Books, Inc.
10300 N. Central Expressway, Suite 400
Dallas, TX 75231
www.benbellabooks.com
www.smartpopbooks.com
Send feedback to feedback@benbellabooks.com

Printed in the United States of America
10 9 8 7 6 5 4 3 2

MARY KITCHEN® is a registered trademark of Hormel Foods, LLC, and is being used with permission from Hormel Foods Corporation

Photographs in color insert: photography by Nina Gallant, food styling by Catrine Kelty

All other image credits appear adjacent to the images in the text or at the back of the book.

Library of Congress Cataloging-in-Publication Data is available for this title.
ISBN 978-1-936661-41-1

Copyediting by Cody Dolan
Proofreading by Iris Bass
Cover design by Faceout Studio, Charles Brock
Text design and composition by Faceout Studio, Charles Brock
Printed by Bang Printing

Distributed by Perseus Distribution
http://www.perseusdistribution.com/

For Danny and Noah, the lights of our lives

TABLE OF CONTENTS

Appetizers

Salads

Main Courses

Desserts and Sweets

INTRODUCTION

When we first walked into the offices of Sterling Cooper, metaphorically speaking, we knew *Mad Men* was going to transport us to another time. It wasn't the retro look of the office furnishings or the décor, or even the fashions, though they helped. It was the background chorus of a hundred electric typewriters clicking away.

Mad Men's obsessive attention to period detail also extends to its food: *what* its characters eat and drink, *how* they eat and drink it, and *where*. We grew up in the 1960s just a few miles from Manhattan, so many of the foods and kitchen and restaurant scenes brought back childhood memories. When we saw Betty Draper serve Turkey Tetrazzini and stuffed celery, or Carla, the Drapers' housekeeper, serve potato salad, it was as if we had traveled back to our mothers' kitchens. When the Draper kids watch Don break out another bottle of Canadian Club or the neighbors come over for bridge night, it reminded us of nights we'd sneak halfway down the stairs in our pajamas to take a peek at our parents and their friends enjoying cocktails and cards.

Judy has a long track record pairing food and literature in two previous cookbooks she co-authored, which naturally extended to curiosity about the food in *Mad Men*. But when friends learned we were writing a *Mad Men*–themed cookbook, many were surprised: there was *food*? All they seemed to remember was a lot of drinking, and maybe Betty making breakfast or dinner in her kitchen.

But there is plenty of food in *Mad Men*. Sometimes it's front and center, but often it's a background detail, the visual equivalent of those clicking typewriters, but a detail that lends great authenticity. Think of Don and Roger Sterling's power lunch at the Grand Central Oyster Bar; Don and Bobbi Barrett's intimate dinner conversation while waiting for their steak tartare at Sardi's; and the buffet tables laden with holiday treats the staff dances past at the Sterling Cooper Draper Pryce Christmas Party. When you saw Joan Harris' Hawaiian-themed New Year's Eve repast, or Betty's Around the World Dinner, didn't you want to pull up a chair?

Our goal was to create a cookbook with recipes for food and drink that either appear in *Mad Men*, or were served in the 1960s by the bars and restaurants featured in the show. We were delighted by the eagerness of many of those establishments to contribute recipes and photographs to this book. For example, since Don and Roger Sterling ate there, The Grand Central Oyster Bar's recipe for Oysters Rockefeller has changed, but thanks to owner and executive chef Sandy Ingber we've been able include the version they would have been served. Sometimes tried-and-true recipes have survived the past half-century: the Caesar Salad at Keens Steakhouse remains the same, as does Sardi's Steak Tartar. Occasionally, we had to go digging for information on a cocktail or dish no longer on the menu: the Beverly Hills Hotel identified and sent us the recipe for a cocktail Pete Campbell sips poolside as a Royal Hawaiian, a cocktail they haven't served since the 1960s. There are times when we aren't shown what the characters are eating, as is the case when Don and Bethany Van Nuys dine at the elegant Barbetta restaurant near Times Square. Barbetta owner Laura Maioglio contributed two recipes that were on the menu in the early 1960s and which Don and Bethany might have enjoyed.

We also wanted to remain true to the manner in which the food and drink we selected would have been prepared in the early 1960s, though we did occasionally use an appliance first introduced in the early 1970s: a food processor.

Period authenticity becomes even more delicious when you have some historical context on the side—information about the restaurants, hotels, foods, chefs, and real-life personalities that feature in *Mad Men* or that shaped the culinary landscape of the times. For example, Beef Wellington was a favorite of President and Mrs. Kennedy, and their White House once served Avocado Mimosas at a state dinner for the president of Pakistan in 1961. There are recipes here for both. We explore how public fascination with the 50th state, Hawaii, translated not just into the hula hoop craze and singer Don Ho's stardom, but the popularity of Polynesian-themed restaurants, cocktails, and foods, and we include recipes for several of them. And you can't fully appreciate the presence of French restaurants and cuisine in *Mad Men* without understanding the revolution in American culinary tastes spawned by the 1961 publication of Julia Child's *Mastering the Art of French Cooking* (Alfred A. Knopf).

We pored over hundreds of cookbooks, magazines, and advertisements from the 1950s and 1960s in our pursuit of information and ideas. To be true to the era, we looked for cookbooks the characters might have used. When Joan Harris (formerly Holloway) made that crown roast in her tiny kitchen to serve at a dinner party, we turned to *The Small Kitchen Cookbook* by Nina Mortellito (Walker and Company, 1964) for a recipe. When Pete Campbell asks his new wife to make rib eye in the pan, we thought a logical cookbook selection for Trudy cooking for her "ad man" would have been *The Madison Avenue Cookbook* by Alan Koehler (Holt, Rinehart and Winston, 1962).

Those cookbooks and magazines took us back to the 1960s and not only helped us choose and develop recipes, but enhanced our appreciation of how various food-related chores and even the different cocktails men and women favored tended to be gender-specific.

Which brings us to those cocktails. There are times when Sterling Cooper might aptly be renamed the Bureau of Alcohol, Tobacco and Firearms (minus the firearms, though who knows *what* Bert Cooper keeps in his desk). The establishments frequented by Don Draper and his colleagues provided many of the cocktails for this book. For example, the recipes for a Sidecar and a Vesper come courtesy of P.J. Clarke's, where Peggy Olson and others from Sterling Cooper celebrate her early copywriting success, and the Manhattan from the Oak Bar, where Don and Roger sometimes stopped for a drink.

To ensure an authentic *Mad Men* experience, every recipe is introduced through a specific scene in the show. And to enhance your enjoyment of the food and drink we scoured period cookbooks and magazines for tips on throwing a successful cocktail or dinner party. We also compiled a small guide to some of the restaurants and bars frequented by *Mad Men* characters. On your next trip to New York, stop by and tell them Don sent you.

We, and a small army of volunteer recipe testers, cracked hundreds of eggs, baked at least a hundred pounds of butter and sugar into various pies and cakes, and poured gallons of gin, vodka, and whiskey, as we tested and retested recipes for this book (even when some didn't *need* retesting). We carved crown roasts and hams, shucked dozens of oysters, and peeled pounds of potatoes, too. So, we can vouch for both the authenticity and the tastiness of the food and drink on these pages. Whether you like to cook, eat, drink, or simply enjoy devouring all things *Mad Men*, our hope is that this book will enhance your appreciation of the show and enrich your understanding of the times in which it is set.

— *Judy Gelman and Peter Zheutlin*

A FEW WORDS ABOUT COCKTAILS

Though the Don Drapers and Roger Sterlings of the 1960s carried themselves with an air of worldly sophistication, they were not sophisticated about liquor, according to Robert Hess, co-founder of the Museum of the American Cocktail in New Orleans. Their brand preferences were more apt to be the result of savvy marketing, a notion Don would appreciate, than the nuances of the product. Cocktails in the 1960s tended to be relatively unsophisticated concoctions (faux Polynesian cocktails such as the Mai Tai had many ingredients but weren't necessarily sophisticated) and, as we often see in the offices of Sterling Cooper, alcohol was often consumed straight out of the bottle into a glass, or "neat." Just as a restaurant of the 1960s could make a basic steak its claim to fame, its martini might be widely praised simply because it was strong, not because it was well made, according to Hess. People often saw cocktails more as alcohol delivery vehicles than as a cuisine, and mixing drinks more like a trade than an art form. The 1990s brought a cocktail revival and people rediscovered and improved upon the classics such as the Old Fashioned, the martini and the Manhattan by paying attention to the attributes of particular whiskeys and vermouths, for example. As with wine and coffee, the past twenty to thirty years has seen an evolution in the appreciation of the art of mixing a fine cocktail.

Though attitudes about cocktails have evolved significantly since the 1960s, these tips for preparing and serving cocktails gleaned from books and magazines of the period will help kick your *Mad Men* cocktail party into high gear and remain good, basic advice. There are additional tips on stocking your liquor cabinet on page 113.

GLASSES

- You're not likely to have each and every type of cocktail glass, but you can make do with a few basics:

  - A martini glass (also called a cocktail glass) is the classic "birdbath" glass; an inverted triangular-shaped bowl on a stem.

  - An Old Fashioned glass (also known as a rocks glass or lowball glass) is a squat, straight-sided tumbler that typically holds 8 or 10 ounces, and is essential for drinks on the rocks because it allows all of the liquid to come in contact with the ice.

  - Highball and Collins glasses are both similar to an Old Fashioned glass, but taller and narrower, with a Collins the taller of the two.

  - Sour glasses are tulip-shaped or straight-sided, 4–6 ounce glasses.

- Chill your cocktail glasses before guests arrive. This not only helps chill drinks quickly, it's classy. And chilling glasses has a psychological impact, too: chilled glasses impart an added sense of refreshment, whether real or perceived. To chill glassware, refrigerate for 30 minutes or freeze for 10. If you don't have space in your refrigerator, either fill glasses with crushed ice and let stand for 5 minutes, then empty and dry, or fill with ice cubes and add water, let stand for 3–4 minutes, then empty and dry.

- To frost a rim with salt or sugar, rub a wedge of citrus fruit around rim or dip rim in water, juice, or liquor and shake off excess. Dip rim into salt or sugar.

TOOLS

Your well-equipped bar should include the following:

- standard cocktail shaker (three-piece stainless steel set comprising shaker cup, built-in strainer, and cap.)

- mixing glass (any container used for mixing cocktail ingredients)

- tall mixing spoon

- coil-rimmed strainer

- muddler (a wooden tool for mashing cherries and other fruit)

- tongs

- fruit squeezer

- small, sharp knife for slicing fruit

- cocktail toothpicks for fruit, olives, and other garnishes

- swizzle sticks

ICE

- Make plenty of ice cubes in advance. If making punch, chill a block of ice the day before. Nothing puts a damper on a cocktail party more than a lack of ice.

- Before adding liquid, crack the ice cubes: place cubes in a heavy-duty plastic bag and tap gently with a hammer. Cracked ice will chill drinks faster. If you have excess water in the glass after adding the crushed ice, drain before adding other ingredients.

- If a recipe calls for shaved or crushed ice, wait until you are ready to mix to prepare the ice as it melts very quickly.

MIXING

- Mixing drinks by hand in a cocktail shaker or mixing glass is preferable to using a blender because blending with ice tends to add more water and dilutes the drink. Shake ingredients vigorously for 10–15 seconds (any longer and the ice begins to melt, leaving the drinks watery).

- A good cocktail should be neither too strong nor too weak. Follow recipe instructions precisely for best results.

- If several guests are having the same cocktail, make them in a batch rather than individually. They'll stay cooler longer.

- If the recipe calls for granulated sugar, use superfine granulated sugar and dissolve it with liquid before adding ice. Simple syrup can be used as a sweetener in many cocktails in lieu of sugar, and mixes more easily than sugar as alcohol is not an efficient sugar solvent. You can purchase simple syrup or make it yourself by combining one cup of superfine sugar and one cup of water in a small saucepan. Place over medium heat and stir until boiling, Reduce heat and simmer for 3–4 minutes, stirring occasionally. Let syrup cool to room temperature.

Leftover syrup can be spooned into a jar and stored up to three weeks in refrigerator.

- With the exception of a self-serve punch, cocktails should be consumed immediately after they are mixed, before they warm and ingredients settle.

DON'S OLD FASHIONED AND ROGER'S MARTINI

SEASON 1, EPISODE 1
"Smoke Gets in Your Eyes"

Mad Men opens in a smoky bar, with Don Draper making notes on a napkin, an empty cocktail glass on the table. He's jotting down ideas for promoting Lucky Strike cigarettes, one of Sterling Cooper's most important clients. When the waiter asks if he'd like another drink, he replies, "Yeah, do this again. Old Fashioned, please."

An Old Fashioned: it's the very first food or beverage mentioned in *Mad Men*, and this popular cocktail makes many appearances in the series. It's Don's drink of choice. And Roger Sterling, with whom Don does a fair share of drinking? He's a martini man.

The unidentified restaurant where Don and Roger get loaded and down dozens of oysters later in the first season could well be the Grand Central Oyster Bar (see Grand Central Oyster Bar's Oysters Rockefeller, page 82), so we turned to this legendary Manhattan eatery for the recipes for these classic cocktails. The Oyster Bar still serves them in the classic 1960s style, too: the martinis are served in small martini glasses because, as manager Jonathan Young explained to us, the martini gets too warm in a larger glass. (The trend to larger martini glasses simply reflects Americans' penchant for bigger is better.) And the Oyster Bar mixes an Old Fashioned just as Don does: they muddle (mash) the fruit.

OLD FASHIONED

At the country club where Roger and Jane Sterling are hosting a Kentucky Derby–themed garden party (season 3, episode 3; "My Old Kentucky Home"), Don meets a man named "Connie" looking in vain for bourbon behind an untended bar. (Unbeknownst to Don, Connie is Conrad Hilton, the hotelier.) As Don goes about making two Old Fashioneds, he asks Connie if rye is okay. But whether you prefer your Old Fashioned with bourbon or rye, to muddle or not to muddle, *that* is the question.

An Old Fashioned typically includes sugar (dissolved with a little water), bitters, bourbon or rye, a thin slice of orange, and a cherry. When the Drapers' neighbors, Carlton and Francine Hanson, come over for cards one evening, daughter Sally makes the drinks. As she hands Don and Carlton their Old Fashioneds, Don has a little critique of Sally's style. "Muddled," he instructs. "That means smash it" (season 2, episode 2; "Flight 1"). And when Don makes

Old Fashioneds for himself and Connie he muddles the fruit. Some think muddling the fruit imparts too much sweetness to the drink, but it's obviously Don's preferred method.

The earliest recipes for what would one day evolve into the Old Fashioned date to the early 1800s, and legend has it that the drink by that name first appeared at the Pendennis Club in Louisville, Kentucky, which explains why bourbon would have been the whiskey of choice. But when it comes to whiskey, Don's preferred brand is Canadian Club. (Canadian Club uses the Scottish spelling, *whisky*, though the American usage is *whiskey*.)

There are many types of whiskey. Bourbon is a corn-based spirit distilled to no more than 160 proof (80% alcohol) and aged at least two years. Tennessee whiskey is similar, but is filtered through sugar maple and charcoal. Rye makes a lighter-flavored but full-bodied whiskey and is often blended with other whiskeys to make a final product. Such blended whiskeys are often simply called rye despite the additional ingredients. Canadian Club is such a blended whiskey, made of corn, rye, rye malt, and barley distillates. Almost all whiskeys are aged for years in charred wooden barrels to add flavor and are typically 80 to 100 proof.

A VINTAGE BOTTLE OF CANADIAN CLUB WHISKY, CIRCA 1960

There have been numerous variations in Old Fashioned recipes over the years, with much attention paid to how to dissolve the sugar: some say water, others seltzer, and still others the bitters. The first recipe calling for orange and cherry together, as part of the recipe and not simply a garnish, appeared in 1933, but various recipes have incorporated orange curaçao, pineapple, lemon peel, simple syrup (instead of sugar), and even absinthe.

There is no absolutely definitive Old Fashioned recipe, but we wanted to provide the Old Fashioned as Don liked it, with his "beloved rye," as Roger once described it (season 1, episode 7; "Red in the Face"), and think the Grand Central Oyster Bar hit the oyster on the shell, so to speak, with this one.

Old Fashioned

COURTESY OF THE GRAND CENTRAL OYSTER BAR, NEW YORK, NEW YORK

NOTE: Bourbon or rye may be used in the Old Fashioned. Rye was originally used, and the Grand Central Oyster Bar is starting to use rye again in these drinks; they use Michter's, but Don would likely choose Canadian Club, the brand we often see in his office and home. Seagrams V.O. and Crown Royal were also popular in the 1960s, says Jonathan Rogers of the Grand Central Oyster Bar.

1 orange slice
1 maraschino cherry
1 teaspoon sugar
Few drops of Angostura bitters
A splash of soda water to muddle ingredients
2½ ounces rye or bourbon

1. In a mixing glass, muddle orange slice, cherry, sugar, bitters, and a little soda water: push around and break up cherry and orange until flavor is released.

2. Add soda water so cherry is wet and sugar is melted. Add rye or bourbon and serve over rocks, if desired.

YIELD: 1 DRINK

See color insert.

MARTINI

Unless you count the olives, a traditional martini only has two ingredients, gin and vermouth. There is some flexibility, however, as some have gin and both dry and sweet vermouth, while others include a pearl onion and/or a lemon twist. Flavored martinis, which a traditionalist such as Roger likely would have abhorred, have also appeared since the days of *Mad Men*: chocolate, pear, apple, and pomegranate, among them.

A PERFECT ASHTRAY FOR THE DESK OF DON DRAPER

As with so many cocktails, the origins of the martini are, well, muddled. One legend has it that the martini originated in a Martinez, California, saloon in 1870; another says that a man named Martini di Arma di Taggia first mixed gin, vermouth, and orange bitters, chilled them on ice, and strained them into a chilled glass at New York's Knickerbocker Hotel in 1911. But the name martini first appeared in the *New and Improved Bartending Manual* published in 1888, lending some credence to the first story and seeming to disprove the second.

Arcane debates aside, our aim was to find a martini Roger would have savored. Since he and Don certainly seemed to be enjoying the drinks served with their oysters, it's fitting that we've used the Grand Central Oyster Bar's martini recipe, as well.

Martini

COURTESY OF THE GRAND CENTRAL OYSTER BAR, NEW YORK, NEW YORK

NOTE: Serve in a small martini glass and put leftovers in a rocks glass.

⅛ *ounce dry vermouth*
2½ *ounces gin*

1. Fill a martini glass with water and large ice cubes (enough to keep it cold while mixing drink).

2. Pour vermouth and gin into a mixing glass and stir.

3. Pour ice and water out of martini glass. Pour martini from mixing glass into martini glass.

YIELD: 1 DRINK

See color insert.

TRADER VIC'S MAI TAI
SEASON 1, EPISODE 1
"Smoke Gets in Your Eyes"

Blue waves gently lapping a golden beach on a remote Polynesian island. Native women swaying their hips in grass skirts. Trade breezes ruffling the palms. The Mai Tai cocktail summons all of those tropical images, but this mainstay of Chinese and Polynesian-themed restaurants, which appears in the very first episode of *Mad Men*, didn't originate in the South Pacific; it was first mixed in Oakland, California.

"We originated this drink; we made the first Mai Tai, we named the drink," wrote Victor Bergeron, better known as Trader Vic, founder of the eponymous restaurant chain, in *Trader Vic's Helluva Man's Cookbook* (Doubleday, 1976). "A lot of bastards all over the country have copied it and copyrighted it and claimed it for their own. I hope they get the pox. They're a bunch of lousy bastards for copying my drink."

Now that we've got *that* straight…

Oddly enough, Bergeron admitted seven years before writing those words that Donn Beach (born Ernest Gantt and known as Don the Beachcomber) had come up with the original Mai Tai. Beach had long claimed to have invented the drink, and Bergeron admitted as much in conversation with Beach and a newspaper columnist. Still, Bergeron's and Beach's versions of the drink are very different. Bergeron's is a sweet-and-sour rum drink with orange curaçao, orgeat syrup, and lime juice (for the sour). Beach's has rum, Cointreau, bitters, falernum (a sweet syrup), and Pernod. (Both have been credited with creating rumaki, as well. For more on Trader Vic, Don the Beachcomber, and rumaki, see Betty's Around the World Dinner: Gazpacho and Rumaki, page 93). Perhaps it's fair to say Bergeron and Beach each invented a drink *called* a Mai Tai, different as their respective recipes are.

Though legend has it that Victor Bergeron was born in the South Pacific and lost a leg to a shark attack as a child (perhaps because that's what he used to tell people who asked), he was born in San Francisco and lost his leg to a childhood illness. Trader Vic's in New York was originally located in the Savoy-Plaza Hotel, where Don and Betty celebrate Valentine's Day 1962 (see Jackie Kennedy's Avocado and Crabmeat Mimosa, page 130), but later moved to its current location, the Plaza Hotel.

According to Bergeron, he was in an Oakland, California, Trader Vic's bar in 1944 and simply decided to try to come up with "the finest drink we could make."

Just as Bergeron was about to taste the new concoction he and his bartender had assembled, friends from Tahiti walked in and he offered to share a first taste with them. After a sip, the woman turned to her husband and asked, "What do you think?" He replied, "It's *mai tai roa áe*," which in Tahitian means "out of this world" or "the best." Bergeron soon brought the cocktail to several popular Hawaiian restaurants and it took off.

When Don Draper and department store heiress Rachel Menken have dinner at the El Morocco on 54th Street (now defunct, but famous in its day for its zebra-patterned wallpaper) Don sticks to the traditional stuff—a whiskey neat this time—but Rachel has a cocktail in a tall glass with a slice of pineapple and a cherry skewered on the handle of a festive cocktail umbrella. "A special Mai Tai," says the waiter.

"That's quite a drink," observes Don.

And indeed it is. Presentation is a big part of the Mai Tai's tropical allure. When made the traditional way, it also packs a wallop like a twenty-foot wave off Waikiki. If big wave surfing isn't your thing, you can always tone a Mai Tai down by increasing the fruit juice or reducing the alcohol; it will still transport you past downtown Oakland all the way to the South Seas.

VICTOR BERGERON, "TRADER VIC," AT WORK AT THE BAR AT HINKY DINKS IN OAKLAND, CALIFORNIA, THE PREDECESSOR RESTAURANT TO TRADER VIC'S. IT WAS HERE THAT HE CLAIMED TO HAVE INVENTED THE MAI TAI IN 1944.

Mai Tai

ADAPTED FROM TRADER VIC'S RUM COOKERY AND DRINKERY
BY VICTOR J. BERGERON (DOUBLEDAY, 1974)

NOTE: We prefer our Mai Tai with orange juice, which was not in the original version. We've included it here in case you prefer a fruitier drink.

1 *lime*

1 *ounce Jamaican rum*

1 *ounce Martinique rum*

2 *ounces orange juice (optional)*

½ *ounce orange curaçao*

¼ *ounce orgeat syrup*

¼ *ounce rock candy syrup (simple syrup)*

   (see Simple Syrup page 7)

Sprig of mint, for garnish

Fruit stick, for garnish

1. Cut lime in half. Squeeze juice over shaved ice in a cocktail shaker. Reserve one half of lime shell. Add rums, orange juice if desired, orange curaçao, orgeat syrup, and rock candy syrup.

2. Hand-shake ingredients well an pour over shaved ice into Mai Tai (double Old Fashioned) glass. Decorate with the lime shell, fresh mint, and a fruit stick.

YIELD: 1 DRINK

TRADER VIC'S ORIGINAL MAI TAI, THE ULTIMATE SYMBOL OF TIKI CULTURE

THE PIERRE HOTEL IRISH COFFEE

SEASON 1, EPISODE 6

"Babylon"

It doesn't take long for Don Draper and Rachel Menken, the daughter and heir apparent of a Jewish department store owner who comes to Sterling Cooper looking for help to revive their flagging business, to become romantically involved. Unfortunately, the romance ends abruptly when Don asks her to run away with him and she refuses. Eager to see her again, Don calls asking to meet, saying it is strictly business and that he wouldn't have called unless it was urgent. Rachel reluctantly agrees to meet Don for "just lunch" and tells him to meet her the next day at the Tea Room in the Pierre Hotel.

The famed Pierre on East 61st Street, now part of the Taj Hotels Resorts & Palaces, is the setting for several memorable scenes in *Mad Men*. It's where Peggy Olson and Herman "Duck" Phillips have a tryst (season 3, episode 7; "Seven Twenty-Three") and, when the principals of Sterling Cooper maneuver to start their new agency, Sterling Cooper Draper Pryce, they temporarily set up shop in Room 435 of the Pierre (season 3, episode 13; "Shut the Door, Have a Seat").

Don tries to charm Rachel when they meet in the Tea Room, but she reminds him sternly that he said he had urgent business to discuss. To underscore her determination to keep the meeting strictly business, she orders only coffee. "Irish coffee?" asks Don, hoping to take the chill out of their encounter. "Coffee," she replies.

That the Tea Room at the Pierre served Irish coffee may have been one of the fruits of an advertising push that started in 1956 to market Irish whiskey in the United States. As the *New York Times* reported on October 2, 1956, a reception at the Irish Products Center on East 50th Street featured representatives from five of Ireland's biggest distillers and an Irish singer and television personality, Carmel Quinn, who "explained that Irish coffee consists of hot coffee, with sugar and Irish whiskey, topped by whipped cream."

Simple to describe; not as easy to make. According to Andrew F. Smith, editor of *The Oxford Companion to American Food and Drink* (Oxford University Press, 2007), Irish coffee was purportedly invented in 1943 by Joe Sheridan, the chef at the airport in Limerick, Ireland, to soothe exhausted New York–bound passengers whose flight had to return to Limerick because of bad weather. A passenger on the flight brought the recipe back to San Francisco, where he and Jack Koeppler, a bartender at the Buena Vista Hotel, tried to re-create it. At first, the whipped cream kept sinking to the bottom, but then Koeppler eventually met Sheridan and learned the secret: "The coffee must be lightly sweetened, the cream must be both fresh and softly whipped, and the cream must be poured into the hot coffee over the back of a spoon." (The Pierre opts for a similar approach, without the spoon; see recipe below.)

The Pierre of the early 1960s, as you would expect, looked quite different than the Pierre of today, especially since undergoing a $100 million renovation in 2009. The Tea Room is gone, but the hotel's elegant Two E Bar/Lounge still serves what it calls a "Classic Irish Coffee," and graciously shared the recipe with us. If Rachel and Don were to meet again at the Pierre today, we'd definitely recommend she indulge in the Irish coffee. You don't need to be Irish to love Irish coffee!

Irish Coffee

COURTESY OF THE PIERRE HOTEL, NEW YORK, NEW YORK

NOTE: The hotel uses Bushmill's Irish Whiskey, but the drink also works well with John Jameson Irish Whiskey. Any variety of whiskey made in Ireland will suffice, hence the name "Irish Coffee."

> *2 ounces Irish Whiskey (see note above)*
> *3½ teaspoons light brown sugar*
> *4 ounces hot coffee*
> *Whipped cream, for topping*

Stir whiskey, brown sugar, and coffee together in a mug. Add whipped cream on top.

YIELD: 1 DRINK

See color insert.

P.J. CLARKE'S SIDECAR AND VESPER

SEASON 1, EPISODE 8

"The Hobo Code"

Peggy Olson's first copywriting success is an ad for Sterling Cooper client Belle Jolie, a lipstick manufacturer. To celebrate, a gang from the office including Pete Campbell, Ken Cosgrove, Harry Crane, Freddie Rumson, Joan Holloway, Lois Sadler, and the switchboard girls head to P. J. Clarke's on Third Avenue.

An authentic New York "saloon" for 125 years and a favorite haunt of Frank Sinatra's, P. J. Clarke's has long been a popular watering hole and eatery for the rich and powerful, the working man, and the Mad Man. It's where the great songwriter Johnny Mercer wrote "One for My Baby," and the ashes of a favorite patron rest in peace behind the bar.

What might they have been drinking that afternoon as they danced to Chubby Checker and the Twist? We asked Doug Quinn of P. J. Clarke's for his suggestions.

New York Times restaurant critic Frank Bruni calls Quinn "a legend," and "the bartenders' bartender." Quinn has been tending bar at P. J. Clarke's ("the Vatican of saloons," he calls it) on Third Avenue since 2003. He wasn't born until a few years after Peggy Olson's visit, but Quinn tapped his encyclopedic knowledge of classic cocktails and suggested a Sidecar, a mix of brandy, curaçao, and lemon juice, and a Vesper—also called a Vesper martini—made with gin, vodka, and Lillet, a French aperitif wine.

SIDECAR

Quinn wrote to us that a Sidecar, "two parts strong, one part sweet, one part sour, adheres to the Pythagorean formula of a classic cocktail. How well you make a Sidecar is a good indication of how good a bartender you are." Quinn added that, according to legend, the Sidecar was created at Harry's New York Bar, a Paris bistro, by Harry himself and was named for the motorcycle sidecar that conveyed Harry to and from his establishment. "If you substitute rum for brandy," wrote Quinn, "it becomes a drink called 'Between the Sheets.' A far naughtier version of a Sidecar."

Sidecar

COURTESY OF DOUG QUINN, P. J. CLARKE'S NEW YORK, NEW YORK

NOTE: To make a flamed orange twist, take an orange slice, separate the pulp of the fruit from the rind and squeeze the juice from the pulp into the cocktail. Then, take the rind/twist and twist it over a flame next to the cocktail (a bar candle will do). The oil squeezed from the fruit will ignite. Drop twist into the cocktail.

According to Doug Quinn, "You can sugar coat the rim of the glass, for a lady."

>*1½ ounces cognac (Hennessey VS)*
>*¾ ounce Cointreau*
>*1 squeeze (½ ounce) fresh lemon juice*
>*1 squeeze (¼ ounce) fresh orange juice*
>*Flamed orange twist, for garnish*
>*(see note above)*

1. Add cognac, Cointreau, and lemon and orange juices to ice in a cocktail shaker.

2. Shake and serve straight up in a cocktail glass. Garnish with orange twist.

YIELD: 1 DRINK

VESPER

"This cocktail has its origins in Ian Fleming's 1953 *Casino Royale* and is named after femme fatale double agent Vesper Lynd," Quinn wrote to us. "The cocktail never made it to the James Bond movie version…As for Vesper…she killed herself and Bond never sipped the cocktail again." The Vesper, added Quinn, is both appropriate to the *Mad Men* era and timeless.

THE MID-TWENTIETH CENTURY CROWD AT P.J. CLARKE'S

Vesper

COURTESY OF DOUG QUINN, P. J. CLARKE'S NEW YORK, NEW YORK

NOTE: Lillet Blonde is a French apéritif made with wine and brandy.

> *1½ ounces gin (Beefeater)*
> *1½ ounces vodka (Ketel One Citroen)*
> *½ ounce Lillet Blonde*
> *Approximately ⅓ ounce fresh lemon juice*
> *Flamed orange twist, for garnish*
> *(see Sidecar note, page 21)*

1. Add gin, vodka, Lillet Blonde, and lemon juice to ice in a cocktail shaker.

2. Shake and serve straight up in a chilled cocktail glass. Garnish with orange twist.

YIELD: 1 DRINK

CLASSIC ALGONQUIN COCKTAIL
SEASON 1, EPISODE 9
"Shoot"

When Jim Hobart, an executive at the large advertising firm McCann Erickson, tries to lure Don Draper away from Sterling Cooper (see Betty's Turkey Tetrazzini, page 175), he calls Don and suggests a rendezvous at "the Algonquin." He's referring to the Algonquin Hotel on West 44th Street, home of the famed Blue Bar.

Though this meeting never takes place, at least as far as we know, the Algonquin was (and remains) a meeting place for movers and shakers in the business and creative worlds, a place the denizens of Madison Avenue in the early 1960s would have visited frequently.

The famed Algonquin Round Table, for which one the hotel's current restaurants is named, was a group of actors, humorists, newspaper writers, and critics that met at a round table in the Algonquin for lunch every day from 1919 to 1929. Membership was fluid, but included, at one time or another, the sportswriter Heywood Broun, editor of the *New Yorker* Harold Ross, actor and humorist Robert Benchley, actress Tallulah Bankhead, and actor and comedian Harpo Marx.

Bartender Rodney Landers of the Blue Bar, and previously of the Plaza Hotel, recommended the classic Algonquin cocktail as befitting two advertising executives meeting quietly to discuss an employment matter. Made with a "top-shelf rye whiskey base," the drink also includes vermouth and pineapple juice as its two other principal ingredients.

THE LOBBY OF THE ALGONQUIN HOTEL

While Jim Hobart is a very persuasive man, we doubt even a couple of Algonquin cocktails, as fine as they are, would have persuaded Don to jump ship from Sterling Cooper.

Classic Algonquin Cocktail

COURTESY OF RODNEY LANDERS, THE BLUE BAR, ALGONQUIN HOTEL, NEW YORK, NEW YORK

NOTE: Landers recommends using a top-shelf small-batch whiskey.

> *2¼ ounces rye whiskey (see note above)*
> *¾ ounce vermouth*
> *¾ ounce pineapple juice*
> *Lemon twist, for garnish*

1. Pour whiskey, vermouth, and pineapple juice in a cocktail shaker and shake.

2. Strain into a rocks glass. Garnish with a lemon twist.

YIELD: 1 DRINK

PEGGY'S BRANDY ALEXANDER

SEASON 1, EPISODE 11

"Indian Summer"

There are early hints that there isn't going to be a second date for Peggy Olson and Carl Winter, a young truck driver Peggy's mother has fixed her up with, when they go on a first date to a seafood restaurant in Brooklyn. Carl lights Peggy's cigarette and she coughs on the first drag, betraying the air of worldly sophistication she is trying to affect. When Carl orders a Rheingold, a distinctively undistinctive New York–brewed beer popular among the working class, Peggy orders a cocktail, a Brandy Alexander.

Peggy recoils slightly at the first sip, and Carl offers to have it sent back. Peggy demurs, saying she has a friend who lives in the city, referring to Joan Holloway, who orders them for her but that they're usually sweeter.

"So you drive a truck?" asks Peggy, a slight tone of condescension in her voice. When Carl tells Peggy he drives for Wise Potato Chips, she counters that her advertising firm has a potato chip client, Utz.

Carl is anchored by his solid, working class roots in Brooklyn; Peggy is striving to loosen hers. She tells Carl, as if he's never been outside Brooklyn, "There's a bar in Manhattan where the glasses are chilled," but she can't tell Carl what's in the drink she's ordered. "You can act like you're from Manhattan," Carl tells her, "but you don't look like those girls," hitting Peggy right where it hurts.

For some women, in Hollywood films at least, the Brandy Alexander was a gateway to alcoholism. In Edward Blake's *Days of Wine and Roses* (1962), Lee Remick's character, Kirsten Arnesen Clay, begins her descent with Brandy Alexanders. It's not hard to see why, as the cocktail is practically a confection. Some recipes even call for ice cream, and Peggy was clearly expecting something that tasted more like dessert.

Don't be fooled by the Brandy Alexander's creamy sweetness, however. It can pack a punch, much like Carl's slap at Peggy's pretensions.

Brandy Alexander

FROM THE DINER'S CLUB DRINK BOOK
(REGENTS AMERICAN PUBLISHING CORPORATION, 1961).

NOTE: This rendition is called an Alexander Cocktail No. 2. The Alexander Cocktail No. 1 is the original, gin-based Alexander.

> *1 ounce crème de cacao*
> *1 ounce brandy*
> *1 ounce cream*

Combine ingredients with cracked ice in a cocktail shaker and shake well. Strain into a 4-ounce cocktail glass.

YIELD: 1 DRINK

STERLING COOPER JADE AND BACARDI STINGER
SEASON 1, EPISODE 12
"Nixon vs. Kennedy"

After the last of the partners has left the office on election eve in 1960, the staff of Sterling Cooper breaks out the booze as they watch the returns of the presidential race on television. It's a pro-Nixon crowd, and the mood is celebratory. NBC's computer projections show the odds of a Kennedy victory at twenty-two to one. Liquor appears from all corners of the office—vodka, whiskey, red wine—but the supply quickly dwindles so Ken Cosgrove, Harry Crane, and the others must try to figure out where to get more with the liquor stores closed.

"I have a bottle of absinthe in my office," says Paul Kinsey, referring to the high-proof spirit that some believe, mistakenly, has dangerous psychoactive qualities.

Joan Holloway offers to open the supply closet, but warns it's not going to be "the sack of Rome."

"What do we have too much of?" asks Cosgrove.

"Rum, crème de menthe, and dog biscuits," replies Joan.

Soon the water cooler is filled with the deep green crème de menthe, a sweet, mint-flavored alcoholic beverage.

We wanted to offer crème de menthe cocktails that would make the staff of Sterling Cooper swoon. After sampling many, we chose two. The first is a refreshing Jade from *Playboy's Host & Bar Book* by Thomas Mario (1971) because it delivered on its promise of a cocktail that was minty "but not overpowering." Although a Stinger, our second selection, is typically made with crème de menthe and brandy, Bacardi provided us with a version made with crème de menthe and rum, the two ingredients intended for human consumption Joan has on hand. Usually, a Stinger is made with white crème de menthe, but use green if you wish; they taste the same.

We're not sure what else, if anything, the Sterling Cooper staff put in that water cooler, but the sweet concoction surely went a long way toward taking the bitterness out of Nixon's defeat.

Jade

FROM PLAYBOY'S HOST & BAR BOOK *BY THOMAS MARIO (PLAYBOY, 1971)*

1¾ ounces golden rum
½ teaspoons green crème de menthe
½ teaspoon orange curaçao
1½ teaspoons lime juice
1 teaspoon sugar
1 slice lime

1. Add rum, crème de menthe, curaçao, lime juice, and sugar with ice cubes in a cocktail shaker. Shake well.

2. Strain into pre-chilled cocktail glass. Place ice in glass, pour cocktail over ice, and add lime slice.

YIELD: 1 DRINK

Bacardi Stinger

COURTESY OF BACARDI RUM, "BE A DRINK EXPERT" BOOKLET, CIRCA EARLY 1960S

¾ ounce white crème de menthe

1½ ounces Bacardi rum

1. Pour crème de menthe and Bacardi into a shaker or pitcher.
2. Shake or stir well with cracked ice. Strain into a cocktail glass and serve.

YIELD: 1 DRINK

BRIDGE NIGHT TOM COLLINS

SEASON 2, EPISODE 2
"Flight 1"

On the night Betty and Don Draper's neighbors, Carlton and Francine Hanson, come over to play bridge, Don puts Sally to work as the bartender. She makes Don and Carlton Old Fashioneds (see Don's Old Fashioned and Roger's Martini, page 9), and when Don tells her to get a drink order from the wives, she reports back, "Two Tom Collins."

"Okay," replies Don, "you don't smash the cherry on that. Just plop it in at the end. Try to keep it in the top of the glass. Gin." Though recipes for the Tom Collins vary, basic ingredients include gin, lemon juice, and sugar or sweet syrup.

There are two oft-repeated stories about the invention of the Tom Collins, the more colorful being that the cocktail owes its origins to the Great Tom Collins Hoax of 1874. In a tradition that began in New York taverns and spread elsewhere shortly afterward, one patron would ask another, "Have you seen Tom Collins?" The inquirer would then suggest that Tom Collins had been speaking ill of his companion and urge him to find Collins and stop him from spreading unflattering rumors. As frantic men searched the bars for the slandering Collins, they'd ask bartenders if they'd seen him and be served a drink that some clever bartender began calling a Tom Collins. Newspapers joined in the hoax, publishing false sightings of the elusive Collins. Just two years later, the first recipe for a drink called a Tom Collins appeared in the 1876 edition of the *Bar-Tenders Guide or How to Mix Drinks* (first published in 1862) by New Yorker Jerry Thomas, someone who would surely have been familiar with the hoax.

The other story is that the Tom Collins is named for a John Collins, the head waiter at a London restaurant named Limmer's. His name appears in a poem that predates the Tom Collins hoax, though the poem is of dubious provenance and the Gin Punch served by Limmer's was not at all like a Tom Collins:

> *My name is John Collins, head waiter at Limmer's,*
> *Corner of Conduit Street, Hanover Square,*
> *My chief occupation is filling brimmers*
> *For all the young gentlemen frequenters there.*

None of this would have mattered to Sally, of course. She just wanted to mix this sweet-and-sour drink correctly and please her parents. Pleasing Carlton probably wasn't as hard. As Francine once told Betty, "He's so stupid he'll drink anything" (season 1, episode 13; "The Wheel").

Tom Collins

ADAPTED FROM GROSSMAN'S GUIDE TO WINE SPIRITS AND BEERS
BY HAROLD GROSSMAN (SCRIBNER, 1964)

NOTE: Powdered sugar was more common in the mid-twentieth century but today is often replaced with simple syrup. For an old-fashioned touch, we chose this recipe because it calls for powdered sugar.

1½ ounces dry gin
1 ounce lemon juice
1 teaspoonful powdered sugar
½ lime
Club soda (about 3 ounces)
Maraschino cherry, for garnish
Orange slice, for garnish

1. Add gin, lemon juice, and powdered sugar to cracked ice in a cocktail shaker and shake thoroughly. Strain into a Collins glass.

2. Add ice cubes, squeeze lime into drink, and fill with club soda. Stir a little and garnish with lime shell, cherry, and orange slice.

YIELD: 1 DRINK

It's easy to lose track of how many Bloody Marys, or Virgin Marys (a Bloody Mary without the vodka), appear in *Mad Men*: on the conference table at Sterling Cooper for morning meetings, at restaurants, and when the Drapers' bartender in residence, young daughter Sally, makes Bloody Marys for her parents one Sunday morning. She goes very heavy on the vodka and light on the tomato juice, but Don doesn't so much as flinch as he downs his first sip.

The Bloody Mary, sometimes called a Red Snapper, is the quintessential "before noon" or brunch cocktail. It's typically spiced with Tabasco and Worcestershire sauces, and sometimes even horseradish. And when garnished with large olives and a shrimp, as they are at New York's famed Oak Bar, the Bloody Mary is practically a breakfast by itself.

"Few cocktail recipes are as laden with lore as the Bloody Mary," writes Anthony Giglio in *Cocktails in New York: Where to Find 100 Classics and How to Mix Them at Home* (Rizzoli, 2004). As Giglio tells it, a Paris barman named Fernand Petoit accidentally mixed vodka and tomato juice and refused to name the drink. A Chicago entertainer who happened to be at the bar said the drink reminded him of a woman named Mary he knew from a Chicago club called Bucket of Blood, hence the name. However, some say Petoit named the drink either for a girlfriend or for Mary Tudor, the sixteenth-century Catholic queen of England who, in returning England to Catholicism, had 300 dissidents burned at the stake, thus earning the nickname "Bloody Mary." When Petoit moved to New York and starting tending bar at the St. Regis Hotel (where Pete Campbell plans to meet a potential client in season 3, episode 13; "Shut the Door, Have a Seat"), he embellished the cocktail with salt, pepper, lemon juice, and Worcestershire sauce and renamed it the Red Snapper. Patrons preferred the original name, and so it stuck.

Others doubt the Petoit story, which dates to the early 1920s. Tomato juice wasn't commercially available until years after Petoit supposedly mixed it with vodka, and making homemade tomato juice was notoriously difficult. Andrew F. Smith, the editor of *The Oxford Companion to American Food and Drink* (Oxford University Press, 2007), points to two other possible origins. The first is that Henry Zbikiewicz, a bartender at New York's '21' Club, invented the cocktail in the 1930s. The other is that comedian George Jessel, a denizen of the '21' Club, was its creator.

The first published Bloody Mary recipe appears in Lucius Beebe's *The Stork Club Bar Book* (Rinehart and Co., 1946). (See Stork Club Cocktail, page 37.) In the December 3, 1939 edition of the *New York Herald Tribune* Beebe wrote, "George Jessel's newest pick-me-up...is called a Bloody Mary: half tomato juice, half vodka." When Smirnoff Vodka placed the first national ad for a Blood Mary in 1955, it featured Jessel claiming to be its inventor. It was at that point that the Bloody Mary really took off, and it has remained popular ever since.

We offer two '21' Club Bloody Mary recipes. The "traditional" recipe is from *The '21' Cookbook: Recipes and Lore from New York's Fabled Restaurant* by Michael Lomonaco with Donna Forsman (1995). At the height of the cocktail's popularity, after the Second World War, '21' often served more than 100 of them before lunchtime every day. It's still a '21' favorite today but bartender Tara Wright, who supplied our second recipe, blends the Bloody Mary mix in a batch and adds it to a glass with vodka over rocks rather then making each drink in-dividually. Her method is especially convenient if you're mixing for a group. She also adds lemon juice and olive brine to the mix, a lime wedge for garnish, and, if desired, half an ounce of horseradish to each individual cocktail. Either way, a '21' Bloody Mary is a great way to start your day and a Mad Man's breakfast of champions.

THE '21' CLUB BLOODY MARY

'21' Traditional Bloody Mary

FROM THE '21' COOKBOOK: RECIPES AND LORE FROM NEW YORK'S
FABLED RESTAURANT *BY MICHAEL LOMANACO WITH DONNA FORSMAN (BROADWAY, 1995)*

1½ ounces vodka

2 ounces tomato juice, chilled

Dash of Worcestershire sauce

Dash of celery salt

Dash of Tabasco sauce

Salt and freshly ground black pepper, to taste

Add ingredients to a shaker filled with ice. Shake well and
pour into a chilled cocktail glass.

YIELD: 1 DRINK

'21' Club Bloody Mary

COURTESY OF BARTENDER TARA WRIGHT, THE '21' CLUB, NEW YORK, NEW YORK

For the Bloody Mary mix

> 24 *ounces tomato juice*
>
> 1¼ *ounces Worcestershire sauce*
>
> 4–5 *drops Tabasco sauce*
>
> ⅛ *teaspoon salt*
>
> ⅛ *teaspoon fresh ground black pepper*
>
> 1 *tablespoon fresh lemon juice*
>
> ½ *tablespoon olive brine*

For the drink

> 2 *ounces vodka*
>
> *Lime wedge*
>
> ½ *teaspoon horseradish (optional)*

1. Make Bloody Mary mix: Mix tomato juice, Worcestershire sauce, Tabasco, salt, pepper, lemon juice, and olive brine in a large container. Taste and adjust as needed.

2. Make the drink: Pour vodka over rocks in a highball glass. Fill glass with Bloody Mary mix. Stir. Garnish with a lime wedge. Add horseradish, if desired.

YIELD: 1 DRINK

STORK CLUB COCKTAIL
SEASON 2, EPISODE 7
"The Gold Violin"

The famed gossip columnist Walter Winchell once called the Stork Club on 53rd Street near Fifth Avenue, "New York's New Yorkiest place." Opened in 1929, the Stork Club became the hub of New York society and attracted movie stars, aristocrats, showgirls, and business moguls. Money, power, and glamour mixed at the Stork Club as in no other place in New York, and its air of exclusivity made it all the more appealing.

"The Stork club's drinking…has been drinking in the grand manner, guzzling with a panache of chic and elegance, a hoisting of crystal chalices in the secure knowledge that the wit, beauty, chivalry, and weather of the world were doing the identical thing at adjacent tables, each one was a location of distinction and reserved for names that make news," wrote the noted author, scholar, socialite, fashion plate, and bon vivant Lucius Beebe (dubbed "Luscious Lucius" by Winchell) in the purple prose that characterized his *Stork Club Bar Book* (1946). Indeed, among the legions of the rich and famous to frequent the Stork Club were Grace Kelly, Charlie Chaplin, Lucille Ball, Bing Crosby, Frank Sinatra, Elizabeth Taylor, the Kennedys…and Sterling Cooper's own Don Draper and his stunning wife, Betty.

When comedian Jimmy Barrett seals a deal for his new television show with ABC, the Stork Club hosts the celebration. Since Don helped Jimmy and his wife, Bobbi, who is also Jimmy's business manager and Don's paramour, get this big break, Jimmy invites him to the party. Smitten with Betty, Jimmy finds a private moment with her while their spouses and an ABC executive talk shop. When Jimmy suggests in no uncertain terms that he believes Don and Bobbi are having an affair, Betty walks away in disgust.

For nearly four decades, the Stork Club was the hub of New York's "café society," a term Beebe coined to describe the elite who frequented the city's popular night spots. To toast Jimmy's future success, we offer the Stork Club Cocktail.

Stork Club Cocktail

FROM THE STORK CLUB BAR BOOK *BY LUCIUS BEEBE (RINEHART AND CO., 1946)*

NOTE: This cocktail also makes a wonderful punch. To serve, multiply ingredients and pour into a punch bowl over a block of ice.

> *Dash of lime juice*
> *Juice of half an orange*
> *Dash of triple sec*
> *1½ ounces gin*
> *Dash of Angostura bitters*

1. Pour ingredients into a cocktail shaker.

2. Shake well, and strain into a chilled 4-ounce cocktail glass.

YIELD: 1 DRINK

DINERS AND DANCERS AT THE WORLD-RENOWNED STORK CLUB ON EAST 53RD STREET

THE BAR AT THE BEVERLY HILLS HOTEL'S POLO LOUNGE

THE BEVERLY HILLS HOTEL ROYAL HAWAIIAN

SEASON 2, EPISODE 11

"The Jet Set"

Don Draper and Pete Campbell arrive in California for a convention of aerospace manufacturers in Los Angeles, but Don abruptly takes off for Palm Springs with Joy, a beautiful young woman he's just met, without a word to Pete. (See Palm Springs Chile Rellenos, page 98.) Pete is dumbfounded and improvises his way through meetings with potential clients.

If you have to be left in the lurch as Pete was, the Beverly Hills Hotel isn't a bad place to be stranded. A haven for the rich, the beautiful, and the famous, it has been the place to see and be seen in L.A. for nearly a century. Located on famous Sunset Boulevard, the hotel marks its centennial in 2012, and its famed Polo Lounge, opened in 1941, has been a hangout for the likes of Frank Sinatra, Dean Martin and the rest of the so-called Rat Pack, Hollywood icons such as Raquel Welch, and the movers and shakers of the entertainment industry. Hotel guests have included Charlie Chaplin, Elizabeth Taylor, and John Belushi, and the hotel has also been an on-location set for several films, including *Designing Women* starring Gregory Peck and Lauren Bacall, and Neil Simon's *California Suite*.

**THE BEVERLY HILLS HOTEL
ROYAL HAWAIIAN**

As Pete relaxes by the hotel pool and makes a phone call to try and rearrange a meeting scheduled in Pasadena (Don's still AWOL and Pete doesn't drive), he has a yellow fruity-looking cocktail at his side and we set out to determine what it is. Robert Rouleau, Beverage Supervisor of the Beverly Hills Hotel, solved the mystery: It's a Royal Hawaiian. It wasn't an easy puzzle to solve; the drink was fashionable in the '50s and '60s and the Polo Lounge hasn't served one in decades.

Not to be confused with a Blue Hawaii (see Joan's Blue Hawaii, page 60), the Royal Hawaiian belongs to that popular family of tropical drinks that emerged as Hawaii approached statehood in 1959 and American fascination with all things Polynesian reached its peak. Not quite as potent as a Mai Tai (see Trader Vic's Mai Tai, page 14), a Royal Hawaiian is nevertheless the perfect refreshment when your boss takes off for Palm Springs and strands you to survive all by yourself on wits and cocktails alone.

Royal Hawaiian

COURTESY OF ROBERT ROULEAU, BEVERAGE SUPERVISOR, THE POLO LOUNGE AT
THE BEVERLY HILLS HOTEL, BEVERLY HILLS, CALIFORNIA

NOTE: To float the dark rum, hold a spoon with its backside up near the inside edge of the glass. Slowly pour the liquid over the spoon and into the glass. Due to its higher sugar content, you may also pour the dark rum directly on top of the cocktail and it will float.

1½ ounces Bacardi Light (Silver) Rum
2 ounces pineapple juice
1 ounce papaya juice
1 ounce Myers's Dark Rum
1 maraschino cherry
Slice of fresh pineapple

1. Fill a cocktail shaker with ice. Add light rum, pineapple juice, and papaya juice to the shaker and shake well.

2. Strain over fresh rocks. Float the dark rum atop the drink. Garnish with cherry and pineapple.

YIELD: 1 DRINK

As the Drapers drive home following dinner with Roger and Mona Sterling, an intoxicated Betty, head on Don's shoulder, says, prophetically, "Lobster Newburg and gimlets should get a divorce. They're not getting along very well" (season 1, episode 2; "Ladies' Room").

But it was the gimlet Betty orders at a bar in October of 1962, with the world on the brink of nuclear war, that really caught our attention. Separated from Don and newly pregnant with their third child, Betty drops Sally and Bobby off at Don's hotel one evening, then stops at a Manhattan bar on the way home. The Cuban Missile Crisis was intensifying by the hour and no one knew whether they'd be waking up the next day or, if they did, what the world around them might look like. Maybe it was the combination of that existential threat and the gimlet that caused Betty to throw caution to the wind and have sex with a handsome stranger in an office at the bar that night. She never even learns his name.

We do know the name of the gimlet's creator, however. Sir Thomas Gimlette, a Royal British Navy surgeon from 1879 to 1913 devised the beverage as a way to get sailors to consume enough lime juice to prevent scurvy.

Our gimlet comes courtesy of New York's '21' Club. If you find yourself needing to meditate (or medicate) in an emergency, sip one slowly, but don't overdo it.

THE '21' CLUB VODKA GIMLET

Vodka Gimlet

COURTESY OF BARTENDER TARA WRIGHT, THE' 21' CLUB, NEW YORK, NEW YORK

NOTE: The drink was created using gin and Rose's Lime Juice. If you switch to fresh lime juice, you'll need to add simple syrup (see page 7) to balance the tartness of the limes.

> **2 ounces vodka**
> **1 ounce Rose's Lime Juice**

1. Add vodka and Rose's Lime Juice to a shaker filled with ice.
2. Shake and strain into martini glass or pour over ice on the rocks.

YIELD: 1 DRINK

RECIPE FOR DISASTER

Early in the first season of *Mad Men*, Betty Draper consults a psychiatrist to help her cope with anxiety and nervousness. One of the first things she says to the doctor is, "I guess a lot of people must come here worried about the Bomb" (season 1, episode 2; "Ladies' Room").

In the 1960s, that meant *the atomic bomb*.

The anxiety, fear, and occasional gallows humor that accompanied the threat of nuclear war are skillfully evoked in several episodes of *Mad Men*, especially when the plot reaches the Cuban Missile Crisis in October of 1962 (season 2, episode 13; "Meditations in an Emergency").

We first see Don Draper watching the televised address in which President Kennedy tells the nation of a build up of Soviet missile sites in Cuba meant to provide nuclear strike capability against the West. When Don comes to the office the next day, small groups of Sterling Cooper employees are huddled around radios, listening to news bulletins. The atmosphere is tense, the employees distracted. Joan Holloway reminds Don that the office has a civil defense protocol and insists the employees have a right to know.

"Trust me," replies Don, "I don't think there will be a point in taking those stairs or diving under a desk."

In their apartment, Trudy and Pete Campbell discuss an escape plan from New York, which Pete finds ludicrous: "If I'm going to die," he says, "I want to die in Manhattan."

The very real threat of nuclear annihilation didn't stop some, including some in the cookbook business, from having fun with the Cold War. In 1969, the *Better Homes and Gardens Guide to Entertaining* contained a recipe for "Bomb Shelter Chocolate-Cherry Delight Cake."

Mixologists had some fun with it, too, and many cocktails were inspired by the lingo of the nuclear age. The B-52, a reference to the U.S. long-range nuclear bomber, contained Kahlúa, Bailey's Irish Cream, and Grand Marnier. An Atomic Fireball was made with rum, Dr. McGillicuddy's Fireball Canadian Whisky, and grenadine. An Atomic Tonic was a mixture of Tanqueray gin, Limoncello, St. Germaine Elderflower Liqueur, and lime juice. A Nuclear Cocktail, served in a chilled shot glass (think Cold War), was made with peppermint schnapps, vodka, and Grand Marnier. There was even a Cuban Missile Crisis cocktail comprising vodka, Bacardi rum, sugar-free lemonade, and grenadine to be served in an Old Fashioned tumbler.

If you had to die in a nuclear attack, you could at least do it in style.

PEGGY AND PAUL'S BACARDI RUM FRAPPÉ
SEASON 3, EPISODE 3

"My Old Kentucky Home"

It's a Friday, but the creative team at Sterling Cooper is going to work the weekend because Bacardi rum executives are arriving Tuesday to see if "Daiquiri Beach," a nascent idea for a Bacardi ad campaign, "has legs." Ken Cosgrove, the account man who handles Bacardi, tells the team Don Draper wants to see copy on Monday morning and artwork by Monday night. Their assignment is to develop five vacation scenarios around the Daiquiri Beach theme. It means Peggy Olson, Paul Kinsey, and Smitty Smith, a relatively new addition to the team hired by Don for his acumen about the youth market, will have to sacrifice their weekend plans.

After Peggy leaves the room where they are brainstorming ideas for Bacardi, Paul calls an old college friend and drug dealer, the unctuous preppy Jeffrey Graves. Peggy returns to a room filled with pot smoke. Paul explains he needs it for inspiration and, after all, "It's Saturday." When Jeffrey asks Peggy her name, she replies, "I'm Peggy Olson and I want to smoke some marijuana."

When her older secretary, Olive Healy, expresses concern about what she's "been doing in there," we see a Peggy Olson who has completely come into her own.

"Don't worry about me," Peggy tells Olive. "I am going to get to do everything you want for me."

While Smitty and Paul engage in post-marijuana banter, Peggy is still turning ideas for Bacardi and Daiquiri Beach over in her head. But it is Paul, we think, who actually hits on the best idea for Bacardi, and he does so *before* Jeffrey arrives with the joints. As he sips Bacardi and Coke and eats an orange, he asks Peggy to get a blender. "Maybe," he says, "we can turn this into a frappé."

The idea may have sounded original to Peggy, Paul, and Smitty, but a recipe for a Bacardi frappé, also called a Daiquiri, appeared in a Bacardi ad as early as August 17, 1953, a decade *before* the Sterling Cooper creative team's weekend brainstorming session. The two-page spread featured "Favorite Rum Recipes from Six Yachtsmen," including one Francisco Fullana of San Juan, Puerto Rico, whose recipe for a frozen Daiquiri calls for blending crushed ice, lime juice, sugar, and Bacardi in a blender and whirling until "thoroughly frappéd." We adapted it for one of two rum frappé recipes that follow. The second variation comes from a ten-page booklet published by Bacardi in the early 1960s called "Be A Drink Expert," and the formula is simpler: it calls for just Bacardi and frozen lemonade or limeade.

When the public learned that President Kennedy's favorite cocktail was a Daiquiri, it became one of the most popular drinks of the era. Call it what you will, a Daiquiri or a Frappé—either way, here's to Peggy getting everything Olive wants for her and more, and to Paul for his not-so-original inspiration! At least he was trying.

Puerto Rican Rum is America's favorite rum—and Bacardi sells more Puerto Rican Rum than all the other brands combined. Bacardi has a distinguished and unique flavor, because it is made by a secret formula known only to members of the Bacardi family.

The following recipes will show you how to use this world-famous liquor to make some of the world's favorite and most delectable cocktails.

The long and the short of it . . .

Bacardi and Cola (Cuba Libre). Pour a jigger of Bacardi over ice cubes in a tall glass. Fill with cola. Squeeze in a little lemon or lime juice.

Bacardi Daiquiri. (The original Daiquiri was made with Bacardi — the best still are.) Put 2 teaspoons of frozen limeade or lemonade concentrate in a shaker or pitcher with ice (or juice of ½ lime or lemon with ½ teaspoon sugar). Add jigger of Bacardi. Shake or stir *well* (the secret of a great Daiquiri). Serve in a cocktail glass or on-the-rocks.

A PAGE FROM A BACARDI PAMPHLET TITLED "BE A DRINK EXPERT," PUBLISHED IN THE EARLY 1960S

Bacardi Rum Frappé

ADAPTED FROM FRANCISCO FULLONO, BACARDI ADVERTISEMENT (AUGUST 1953)

1 cup finely crushed ice
Juice of half a lime (½ ounce)
1 teaspoon sugar
1½ ounces light Bacardi rum

Place all ingredients in a blender and blend until thoroughly frappéd.

YIELD: 1 DRINK

Bacardi Daiquiri

COURTESY OF BACARDI RUM, "BE A DRINK EXPERT" BOOKLET, CIRCA EARLY 1960S

2 teaspoons frozen limeade or lemonade
concentrate
1½ ounces Bacardi rum

1. Pour concentrate into a shaker or pitcher of ice.

2. Add Bacardi rum. Shake or stir well. Serve in a cocktail glass.

YIELD: 1 DRINK

JANE STERLING'S MINT JULEP
SEASON 3, EPISODE 3
"My Old Kentucky Home"

Roger Sterling's hedonism and lack of self-awareness are in full flower at the Kentucky Derby–themed garden party he and his new young wife Jane throw at an elegant Long Island country club. Guests mingle under the party tent and sip mint juleps in silver cups, Southern-style. Made up in blackface, and backed by a jazz band clad in straw boaters and Roaring Twenties–style red-and-white striped jackets, he sings "My Old Kentucky Home" to Jane, the overt racism clearly lost on him and over Jane's head. Later, Don and Betty Draper have to help Jane to her seat; she's clearly had a few too many mint juleps.

This classic Southern cocktail evokes the gentility of the South and hot, humid summer days passed on the porch of an elegant plantation-style home. For Betty, mint juleps were also the perfect refreshment to serve to the adults who accompany their children to Sally's sixth birthday party (season 1, episode 3; "Marriage of Figaro").

The origins of the mint julep aren't known, though legend has it that a Kentuckian boating on the Mississippi River stopped along the banks one day to pick fresh mint, which he then added to his bourbon and water mixture. An integral part of Kentucky culture, the mint julep is the official drink of the Kentucky Derby.

We offer two versions of the mint julep. The first is a contemporary julep courtesy of the '21' Club in Manhattan that features a delicious mint-infused simple syrup. The second is a more classic rendition and comes from *The Stork Club Bar Book* by Lucius Beebe (1946). (For more on Lucius Beebe and the Stork Club see Stork Club Cocktail, page 37.) "This is the Stork julep," wrote Beebe in his introduction to the recipe, "and it has stayed and strengthened many brave men and fair women, confirming them in the almost irrefutable belief that most of the good things of the world come in glass bottles and the very best of them say bourbon on the outside."

Roger couldn't have said it better himself.

'21' Club Mint Julep

COURTESY OF THE '21' CLUB NEW YORK, NEW YORK

Fresh mint leaves
½ ounce fresh lemon juice
1 ounce Mint Simple Syrup (see recipe below)
2 ounces bourbon

1. In a Collins glass, muddle mint leaves in fresh lemon juice and Mint Simple Syrup.

2. Fill glass with crushed ice and add bourbon. Stir. Garnish with a bruised mint leaf.

YIELD: 1 DRINK

MINT SIMPLE SYRUP

Bunch of fresh mint leaves
About 2 cups sugar
Boiling water

1. Crush a goodly bunch of mint leaves in a quart container. Fill to halfway mark with sugar, then fill with boiling water. Stir well to dissolve sugar.

2. Let mint steep while syrup cools. Strain. Let the syrup cool to room temperature and spoon it into a jar. Seal tight and store in refrigerator for up to three weeks.

Stork Club Mint Julep

ADAPTED FROM THE STORK CLUB BAR BOOK
BY LUCIUS BEEBE (RINEHART AND CO., 1946)

4 *sprigs fresh mint, plus extra sprig for garnish*
1 *teaspoon sugar or simple syrup (see page 7)*
2 *ounces bourbon*
Green cherry, if desired

1. Mash mint leaves and sugar or simple syrup with muddler in a silver mug.

2. Fill silver mug with shaved ice and add bourbon. Stir until the outside of the mug is frosted.

3. Decorate with sprig of mint and serve with straws. Add green cherry, if desired.

YIELD: 1 DRINK

See color insert.

THE DUBLIN HOUSE RUSTY NAIL

SEASON 3, EPISODE 6

"Guy Walks into an Advertising Agency"

When Joan's husband, Greg Harris, comes home drunk late one night and breaks the news that he didn't get the chief residency in surgery he'd worked and hoped so hard for, he tells Joan he's been drinking alone at the Dublin House, a neighborhood Irish bar on West 79th Street. Opened in 1921 during Prohibition, the bar looked like an ordinary residence on the outside, but had a full bar and restaurant inside.

The Dublin House Bar and Tap Room wasn't a place for refined cocktails in the early 1960s, according to manager Paula Griffin. It was a favorite of sailors whose ships docked at the 79th Street boat basin; The Dublin House was literally the first place they saw when they disembarked. Sailors and iron workers building Manhattan skyscrapers came for a shot of whiskey and beer, often mixing the two into a mixture known as a Boilermaker and downing them in one long draw. The Dublin House has always opened at 8 a.m. because many of its customers liked to jumpstart their days with a shot or two or three. One of the only cocktails served there at the time was a Rusty Nail, but today the Dublin House also serves top shelf drinks such as martinis.

The Rusty Nail, a mix of whiskey and Drambuie liqueur (often with a twist and usually over ice), has a reputation as a dive bar drink and can be adjusted for sweetness by adding more or less Drambuie; the honey, herbal taste of the Drambuie balances the biting, hot taste of the whiskey.

Drambuie, according to its manufacturer, is an elixir of herbs, spices, and heather honey crafted with aged Scotch whiskeys and was created by Scottish Prince Charles Edward Stuart, better known as Bonnie Prince Charlie, in the mid-1700s. The concoction didn't resurface for more than a century until James Ross, the owner of the Broadford Hotel on the Isle of Skye—a hotel still in operation—began mixing *dram buidheach*, "the drink that satisfies." It was registered in 1893 under the name Drambuie.

Our Rusty Nail cocktail recipe comes to you courtesy of Dr. Greg Harris' refuge of choice, the Dublin House itself.

Rusty Nail

COURTESY OF THE DUBLIN HOUSE BAR AND TAP ROOM, NEW YORK, NEW YORK

1½ ounces whiskey
½ ounce Drambuie

Pour whiskey and Drambuie into a mixing glass and stir. Pour into a rocks glass over ice.

YIELD: 1 DRINK

CANADIAN CLUBHOUSE PUNCH AND LUCKY STRIKE HOLIDAY EGGNOG

SEASON 4, EPISODE 2

"Christmas Comes But Once a Year"

The 1964 Christmas Party at Sterling Cooper Draper Pryce is supposed to be a low-key affair; the firm is struggling and an extravagant celebration is neither in the cards nor the budget. But when Roger Sterling learns that Lee Garner, Jr., the arrogant, party-boy son of Lucky Strike owner Lee Garner, Sr., is going to be in town, they have to pull out all the stops and put on a show. Lucky Strike is the firm's biggest account, Lee loves Christmas, and Roger will do whatever it takes to keep his most important happy.

CANADIAN CLUBHOUSE PUNCH

Nothing says "party" like a festive punch, and if you're throwing one of your own this is the punch to serve, especially if Lee Garner, Jr., is coming. Self-serve punch was a popular feature of parties of all kinds in the 1960s, and since guests often had no idea what was in it, or in what quantities, it sometimes left more than a few of them reeling.

This fruity holiday recipe for Canadian Clubhouse Punch from a 1961 advertisement is sure to get your holiday party or special occasion off on the right foot and keep your guests, or important clients, happy.

The word *punch* is generally thought to be a shortened version of *puncheon*, a cask used to transport rum. Regardless, the alcohol in punch can be brandy, rum, gin, sherry, or whiskey. If you're striving for authenticity, note that Canadian Club didn't produce a whiskey aged twelve years in Don Draper's time, though they do today; the six-year premium whiskey would have been the one on Don's credenza, and in his punch.

Canadian Clubhouse Punch

FROM CANADIAN CLUB ADVERTISEMENT (DECEMBER, 1961)

NOTE: Freeze a block of ice in advance for the punch bowl.

Thin peel of 2 oranges
¼ cup sugar
2½ cups orange juice
6 ounces fresh lemon juice
2 teaspoons orange extract
4 ounces blackberry liqueur or blackberry
   brandy
1 750-milliliter bottle Canadian Club Whisky
Block of ice, for punch bowl
1 orange, thinly sliced in half-moons

1. In a large mixing bowl, mash orange peel and sugar. Add orange juice and lemon juice and stir until sugar dissolves. Add orange extract, liqueur or brandy, and whiskey and stir. Cover and refrigerate for 2–4 hours.

2. Take punch out of refrigerator and remove orange peel with a slotted spoon. Place block of ice in a punch bowl and pour punch into bowl. Float orange slices in bowl, or garnish each punch cup with a slice.

YIELD: ABOUT 2 QUARTS (APPROXIMATELY 12 SERVINGS)

See color insert.

A PAGE FROM A CANADIAN CLUB COCKTAIL BOOK PUBLISHED IN 1956

LUCKY STRIKE HOLIDAY EGGNOG

No Christmas party is complete without eggnog, and there's plenty of it for the partygoers to sip as they await Lee Garner's arrival.

Eggnog is a vestige of America's British heritage. It evolved from the English posset, a hot drink popular in medieval times in which egg yolks and whites are whipped with ale, cider, or wine. In America, cream mixed with rum, brandy, or whiskey became the basis of eggnog. Served at holiday parties since the nineteenth century, eggnog is now a long-running American holiday tradition.

We adapted two eggnog recipes to arrive at this version: one from the *Post-Standard* newspaper of Syracuse, New York (December 8, 1960) and another from a 1964 ad for Puerto Rican rums that declared, "Puerto Rican rums… refuse to be subdued in an eggnog." We've also included a "quickie" version from Bacardi: premade eggnog to which you simply add rum and whipped cream.

However you choose to prepare it, we suggest getting your eggnog before Lee Garner, Jr., shows up. As he says when he does arrive, "I've been drinking all day," and it looks like he's not done yet.

Eggnog

ADAPTED FROM A RECIPE FOR HOLIDAY EGG NOG,
THE POST-STANDARD, SYRACUSE, NEW YORK, DECEMBER 8, 1960

NOTE: Many 1960s eggnog recipes called for using raw eggs; it wasn't until the 1980s that health concerns were raised about consuming raw eggs. This recipe calls for cooked egg yolks. If you prefer to use cooked egg whites as well, combine the whites with the sugar and salt and beat over hot water or over low heat in a heavy saucepan until the whites stand in soft peaks.

6 *eggs separated*
½ *cup sugar, divided*
4 *cups milk or cream*
¼ *teaspoon salt*
2 *cups heavy cream*
2 *teaspoons vanilla extract*
¾–1 *cup spirits such as cognac, brandy, or rum*
Freshly grated nutmeg for topping

1. In the bowl of an electric mixer, beat egg yolks and ¼ cup of sugar until light.

2. Heat milk or cream in a heavy saucepan until it boils. Remove from heat immediately and gradually add small amounts of the milk to the egg yolks, stirring constantly so eggs do not scramble. Pour all of the egg/milk mixture back into saucepan and stir constantly over very low heat until the mixture coats a metal spoon, bubbles at the edges, or reaches 160°F. Place in refrigerator to chill before adding remaining ingredients.

3. Place the egg whites in a bowl of an electric mixer, add salt

and beat until stiff peaks form. Beat in remaining ¼ cup of sugar. Fold egg whites into custard mixture. In the bowl of an electric mixer whip the heavy cream, and fold into the mixture. Add vanilla and spirits and keep chilled until serving. The mixture should be very thick. Chill for at least 3 hours, and dust with nutmeg before serving.

YIELD: ABOUT 20 ½-CUP SERVINGS

The American Egg Board states: *"There have been warnings against consuming raw or lightly cooked eggs on the grounds that the egg may be contaminated with Salmonella, a bacteria responsible for a type of foodborne illness. Healthy people need to remember that there is a very small risk and treat eggs accordingly. Use only properly refrigerated, clean sound-shelled fresh grade A or AA eggs. Avoid mixing yolks and whites with the shell."*

Quick Eggnog

FROM A PUERTO RICAN RUM ADVERTISEMENT, 1964

12 ounces gold or amber label Puerto Rican rum
1 quart prepared eggnog
1 cup whipped cream
Freshly grated nutmeg for topping

1. In a punch bowl, add rum to prepared eggnog.

2. Fold in whipped cream. Chill and dust with nutmeg before serving.

YIELD: 12 SERVINGS

JOAN'S BLUE HAWAII

SEASON 4, EPISODE 3

"The Good News"

On New Year's Eve 1964, Joan Harris (the former Joan Holloway), Sterling Cooper's formidable femme fatale, is dreading the impending deployment of her husband, the insecure, volatile, and sometimes cruel Dr. Greg Harris, to Vietnam. When he returns home from work late that evening, Joan greets him wearing a Hawaiian lei and places one around his neck, as well. "What are you doing up?" Greg asks. Joan replies that she figured they would spend New Year's Eve in Hawaii, and on the table is traditional Hawaiian fare including a fresh fruit salad, a pineapple-glazed ham (see Pineapple-Glazed Ham, page 205), and a cocktail glass filled with a sky blue liquid.

The blue liquid appears to be a Blue Hawaii, a fruity cocktail popular in the 1960s. It derives its color from blue curaçao, a liqueur made from the oil of the dried peels of larahas oranges that grow on the Caribbean island of Curaçao. The oranges aren't blue, of course. Rather, colorants are added to make blue, orange, yellow, and green curaçao. Though the drink makes good use of many traditional Hawaiian flavors, it is not of Hawaiian origin.

As Hawaii statehood approached in August 1959, American fascination with all things Hawaiian, from the hula hoop to Polynesian cuisine, deepened. The hula hoop, like blue curaçao, is not actually Hawaiian. Though people have been using hoops as toys for millennia, the California-based Wham-O Company, makers of the Frisbee flying disk, developed the hula hoop in the late 1950s. Nevertheless, both the hula hoop and blue curaçao came to be associated with Hawaii, mainly through marketing that aimed to take advantage of the public's infatuation with the islands. "Back-Yard Luaus Are Likely to Become as Popular in the U.S. as the Hula Hoop," declared the *New York Times* on March 13, 1959.

America's love affair with Hawaii was reflected in many other ways in the late 1950s and on into the 1960s. Elvis Presley's 1961 film *Blue Hawaii* was followed by two more films that celebrated the fiftieth state, *Girls!Girls!Girls!* in 1962 and *Paradise, Hawaiian Style* in 1965. Hawaiian-born singer Do Ho rose to stardom singing Hawaiian-style songs; the ukulele, a musical instrument of Hawaiian origin, was popularized; and the original *Hawaii Five-O* television series debuted in 1968.

The Blue Hawaii didn't evolve so much as simply burst onto the cocktail scene. According to Jeff Berry, author of *Sippin' Safari: In Search of the Great*

"Lost" Tropical Drink Recipes and the People Behind Them (2007), the Blue Hawaii was invented by Harry K. Yee of Waikiki's Hawaiian Village Hotel "at the behest of the Bols liquor company, which was looking for ways to boost sales of its blue curaçao liqueur."

For Joan's Blue Hawaii (sometimes called a Blue Hawaiian), we adapted recipes from both Berry's *Sippin' Safari* and from a 1969 edition of *Gourmet* magazine, a perfect blend of blends you might say. Either way, a Blue Hawaii will transport you to the tropics, even on a New Year's Eve in New York.

Blue Hawaii

ADAPTED FROM SIPPIN' SAFARI: IN SEARCH OF THE GREAT "LOST" TROPICAL DRINK RECIPES AND THE PEOPLE BEHIND THEM *BY JEFF BERRY (SLG PUBLISHING, 2007) AND* GOURMET *MAGAZINE (JUNE, 1969)*

3 ounces pineapple juice

1½ ounces light rum

1 ounce sweet-and-sour mix (see Homemade Sweet-and-Sour Mix below)

1 ounce blue curaçao

1 ounce lemon juice

1 small cube fresh pineapple, plus a wedge for garnish

1 maraschino cherry, for garnish

1. Pour pineapple juice, rum, sweet-and-sour mix, blue curaçao, and lemon juice into a blender container. Add a small cube of pineapple and mix. Add ½ cup of crushed ice and blend thoroughly.

2. Pour into a punch glass and garnish with a cherry and a small wedge of fresh pineapple.

YIELD: 1 DRINK

HOMEMADE SWEET-AND-SOUR MIX

¾ cup water

¾ cup sugar

½ cup fresh lemon juice

½ cup fresh lime juice

1. Combine water and sugar in medium saucepan. Stir over medium heat until sugar dissolves. Bring to boil. Remove from heat and cool.

2. In a pitcher, combine syrup, lemon juice, and lime juice. Refrigerate until cold.

NEW YORK'S FAMED OAK BAR ON CENTRAL PARK SOUTH

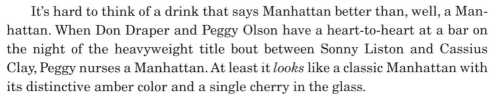

It's hard to think of a drink that says Manhattan better than, well, a Manhattan. When Don Draper and Peggy Olson have a heart-to-heart at a bar on the night of the heavyweight title bout between Sonny Liston and Cassius Clay, Peggy nurses a Manhattan. At least it *looks* like a classic Manhattan with its distinctive amber color and a single cherry in the glass.

Years earlier, Don and Roger Sterling stop by the Oak Bar on Central Park South after work one evening (season 1, episode 7; "Red in the Face"). (The Oak Bar has a Hollywood credit to its credit: it's where Cary Grant's character in Alfred Hitchcock's *North by Northwest*, Roger Thornhill, is kidnapped.) Don is having one of his beloved Old Fashioneds and Roger one of his ubiquitous martinis as they eye the beautiful young women a few bar stools away (see Don's Old Fashioned and Roger's Martini, page 9).

The Oak Bar offered a recipe for one of their signature cocktails for this book, the classic Manhattan they served in the 1960s. Today, the Oak Bar also serves an updated version called the Maker's Manhattan, made with Maker's Mark (a bourbon whiskey), sweet vermouth, and brandied cherries.

As with many cocktails, it is virtually impossible to sort out fact from fiction when trying to discern the origins of the Manhattan. Legend has it the drink was first made for Lady Randolph Churchill, Winston's mother, when she hosted a banquet for presidential candidate Samuel Tilden at the Manhattan Club in the early 1870s. This story has largely been debunked, however. Some say a Manhattan bartender named Black invented it in the 1860s. And *The Oxford Companion to American Food and Drink* (Oxford University Press, 2007) editor Andrew F. Smith says the cocktail was "created by an unknown mixologist," probably in the 1870s. Whatever its origins, the Manhattan is one of the most popular cocktails ever made, and one of the most difficult to make well because everything hinges on both the types of bourbon and vermouth used and how they work in combination. When you taste the Oak Bar's rendition, we think you'll agree they got it right.

Manhattan

COURTESY OF THE OAK BAR, PLAZA HOTEL, NEW YORK, NEW YORK

2 ounces rye whiskey

½ ounce sweet vermouth

2–3 dashes Angostura bitters

Maraschino cherry, for garnish

1. Pour whiskey, vermouth, and bitters into a mixing glass with ice cubes. Stir well.

2. Strain into a chilled cocktail glass. Garnish with the cherry.

YIELD: 1 DRINK

PLAYBOY WHISKEY SOUR

SEASON 4, EPISODE 10

"Hands and Knees"

Sterling Cooper copywriter Paul Kinsey is at his insufferable best when he hosts a party at his Montclair, New Jersey, bachelor pad (season 2, episode 2; "Flight 1"). His neighbors mingle with the younger set from Sterling Cooper, all of them drinking whiskey sours out of glass jars. Paul, clad in an ascot and holding a pipe, strolls around holding a brandy snifter with rum he claims was salvaged from an 1871 shipwreck.

When Pete Campbell asks him why he didn't get an apartment in the Village, Paul tries to paint Montclair as the leading edge of hip. At one point Paul introduces his new girlfriend, an African American woman named Sheila Winter, to Joan Holloway. Later in the episode Joan, with whom Paul has a past, delivers a devastating takedown of Paul and his Bohemian pretensions—including his shipwrecked rum and his attraction to Sheila—but the humble whiskey sour is surely not part of his posturing.

A traditional whiskey sour is a simple mix of whiskey (usually bourbon), lemon juice, and sugar, garnished with an orange slice and a cherry. Many drinkers today know the whiskey sour as a drink made with a commercial pre-made sour "mix," but a traditional whiskey sour, such as the one that appeared in the 1862 edition of Jerry Thomas' *Bar-Tenders Guide or How to Mix Drinks,* would never be made with a commercial mix. Still, the traditional whiskey sour was an unpretentious affair.

The whiskey sour appears again two seasons later, when Lane Pryce's cruel, domineering father, Raymond, comes to town and Lane implores Don Draper to join them for dinner. Lane takes them to the Playboy Club, where Lane's African American girlfriend, Toni Charles, works as a Playboy Bunny. Judy, one of the Bunnies, comes to take their order and Lane asks for three whiskey sours, but the disagreeable Raymond wants iced bourbon instead. So, make it two whiskey sours.

Hugh Hefner's aging Playboy empire is still alive but, while Playboy is widely seen as an anachronism today, in the 1960s it embodied a cool, modern sophistication. In addition to his "lifestyle" magazine and syndicated television shows—*Playboy's Penthouse* (1959–60) and *Playboy After Dark* (1969–70), which were set as parties featuring Playboy Playmates and celebrities at Hefner's penthouse—Hefner owned the famous Playboy Clubs, nightclubs featuring scantily clad Playboy Bunnies as servers. The first Playboy Club opened in

Chicago in 1960, and others soon followed in the United States and elsewhere. The New York club opened in December 1963 on East 59th Street in Manhattan, and so was relatively new when Lane, his father, and Don visited. For men like Lane Pryce, membership in the Playboy Club was a status symbol. Members were called "keyholders," because membership was the key that opened the door to the pleasures of the Playboy lifestyle.

The whiskey sour Lane and Don would have imbibed at the Playboy Club may well be found in *Playboy's Host & Bar Book* by Thomas Mario (1971). Lane should have followed the advice in Mario's book: "Every prearranged drinking session calls for two kinds of alchemy: The first is mixing potables; the second is mixing people." We doubt Raymond Pryce mixed well with anyone; he's about as sour as they come.

ACTOR HUGH O'BRIEN WITH JOY PERCIVAL, "BUNNY JILL," AT A PLAYBOY CLUB IN THE 1960S

Whiskey Sour

FROM PLAYBOY'S HOST & BAR BOOK *BY THOMAS MARIO (PLAYBOY, 1971)*

NOTE: For a more tart drink, reduce the amount of sugar. For a mellower drink, substitute ½ ounce lemon juice and ¼ ounce of orange juice for ¾ ounce of lemon juice.

> *2 ounces blended whiskey*
> *¾ ounce lemon juice*
> *1 teaspoon sugar*
> *½ slice lemon*
> *1 maraschino cherry (optional)*

1. Add whiskey, lemon juice, and sugar to ice in a cocktail shaker and shake well.

2. Strain into prechilled glass. Garnish with lemon slice and cherry, if desired.

YIELD: 1 DRINK

BETTY'S STUFFED CELERY

SEASON 1, EPISODE 3

"Marriage of Figaro"

Some of nature's finest, and simplest, foods come with convenience grown right in. The humble celery stalk is a perfect example. With a natural half-tube shaped groove and a form that's easy to hold and eat, the celery stalk begs for a filling to complement its refreshing taste and firm, snappy texture. Stuffed celery has been a popular appetizer, hors d'oeuvre, and snack since the beginning of the twentieth century, and was a staple of dinner parties throughout the 1960s.

For those with more sophisticated palates, soft cheeses topped with spices such as curry, paprika, or even salt and pepper make an excellent filling. But there's virtually no end to the combinations that make a good celery stuffer: cream cheese and some combination of raisins, nuts, and cranberries; cream cheese and olives; crabmeat, lobster, or chicken salad; chipotle-infused cheddar; or even a mayonnaise, mustard, shredded Swiss cheese, and chopped ham filling.

When Betty Draper prepares hors d'oeuvres to serve to the adults at Sally's birthday party, she fills celery stalks with cream cheese and places them on a tray garnished with decorative leafy greens and red peppers. Concerned that the stuffed celery stalks look too plain, she asks her friend, Francine Hanson, "Capers?"

"You want to pick those out of the rug?" replies Francine.

"Well, they look naked," says Betty of her plain white and green concoction.

This stuffed celery recipe omits capers, so you won't need to pick them out of *your* carpets. Instead, the celery is *fully dressed* with a tasty combination of cream cheese, mayonnaise, stuffed olives, and almonds.

Stuffed Celery

ADAPTED FROM THE GOOD HOUSEKEEPING COOKBOOK *(HEARST, 1963)*

3 *ounces soft cream cheese*

1 *tablespoon mayonnaise*

8 *chopped stuffed olives*

10 *minced, blanched almonds*

4 *long, wide crisp celery stalks*

1. Combine cream cheese, mayonnaise, olives, and almonds in a small bowl.

2. Stuff celery stalks with filling. Chill well. Cut into bite-size pieces or 2–3 inch pieces before serving.

YIELD: ABOUT 8 SERVINGS

CLASSIC SHRIMP COCKTAIL

SEASON 1, EPISODE 4

"New Amsterdam"

One evening Trudy and Pete Campbell join Trudy's well-to-do parents, Tom and Jeannie Vogel, at a Manhattan restaurant for dinner. They begin with appetizers. When Trudy, every ounce Daddy's little girl, announces she has "great news," her mother, delightfully surprised, answers, "Already?" It's not what she thinks. Trudy isn't pregnant; she and Pete have found an apartment they can't afford on 83rd Street. When Tom offers to help with the rent, Pete thanks him but, contrary to Trudy's wishes, says they'd rather wait.

"For what?" barks Tom. "Start your life already. You're gonna be a rich bastard on your own someday and waiting is a bunch of bullshit."

Good advice, especially when you're staring, as Trudy is, at the shrimp cocktail she's ordered.

Appetizers made with shellfish topped with or dipped in a spicy tomato-based sauce and served in small cups were popular in the United States beginning in the late nineteenth and early twentieth centuries, but we owe the *cocktail* in shrimp cocktail to Prohibition in the 1920s. If you couldn't drink a cocktail—not legally, anyway—you could at least eat one and make good use of your stemware in the process.

Oysters (see Grand Central Oyster Bar's Oysters Rockefeller, page 82) were initially the most common shellfish used in such appetizers, but shrimp, less popular at the turn of the twentieth century, was growing in popularity thanks to Cajun and Creole recipes from the Gulf Coast, where Tabasco, a product of Louisiana, was used to liven up the sauce. As shrimp became more commonplace (and the ability to transport them across distances while keeping them fresh improved), the shrimp cocktail—with the shrimp curled around the lip of a cocktail glass—became a nationwide phenomenon. Refreshing, tangy, and light, it's a classic that is still in style. This shrimp recipe is from *The James Beard Cookbook* by James Beard (1961), and the cocktail sauce is from a cookbook often seen on Betty Draper's kitchen counter, *The Better Homes and Gardens New Cookbook* (1962).

Fresh, shelled shrimp, tail on, are the easy part; the magic is in the cocktail sauce. We don't think we're alone in believing that the shrimp are just a vehicle for delivering the savory sauce. But don't wait for Trudy to start. Waiting is… well, Tom said it best.

Classic Shrimp Cocktail

SHRIMP FROM THE JAMES BEARD COOKBOOK *BY JAMES BEARD (DUTTON, 1961);*
COCKTAIL SAUCE FROM BETTER HOMES AND GARDENS NEW COOKBOOK *(MEREDITH, 1962)*

For the shrimp

36 *medium-large shrimp*

1 *thick slice lemon*

3 *sprigs parsley*

1 *peeled onion*

3–4 *peppercorns*

1 *teaspoon salt*

For the cocktail sauce

¾ *cup chili sauce*

2–3 *tablespoons horseradish*

2–3 *tablespoons lemon juice*

1 *teaspoon Worcestershire sauce*

1 *teaspoon grated onion*

¼ *teaspoon salt*

Few drops of Tabasco sauce

Finely chopped celery, optional

Lettuce, for serving, optional

1. Prepare the shrimp: Shrimp may be shelled and cleaned before or after cooking, by peeling off the shell, rinsing off any grit, and removing the black vein down the back. Leave shrimp tails intact.

2. Pour enough water to cover the shrimp in a saucepan. Add lemon, parsley, onion, peppercorns, and salt. Bring to a boil and add the shrimp. Simmer for 3–5 minutes, depending on

the size, until shrimp are pink and cooked through. Do not overcook. Drain and chill shrimp until ready to serve.

3. Make cocktail sauce: Combine all cocktail sauce ingredients in a small bowl. Mix and refrigerate.

4. To serve as individual appetizers, mix shrimp with finely chopped celery (if desired) and serve in lettuce-lined sherbet glasses. For a party snack, fill a large bowl with crushed ice and center with a small bowl of cocktail sauce; arrange shrimp over ice. Top with finely chopped celery (if desired). Serve with wooden picks for dipping shrimp into sauce.

YIELD: 6 SERVINGS

In 1960, the still relatively new state of Israel was looking to boost its tourism industry. Americans, especially Jewish Americans, were infatuated with the Jewish state; Leon Uris' 1958 book *Exodus*, a novel about the birth of Israel, had been a major bestseller in the United States for two years.

In the course of shopping for an advertising agency to launch a major advertising campaign to promote tourism to Israel, two officials from the Israel Ministry of Tourism, Lily Meyer and Yoram Ben Shulai, as well as Nick Rodis, an executive with Olympic Cruise Lines, pay a visit to Sterling Cooper. When Roger Sterling, glib and feckless as always, introduces Yoram to Don Draper as "urine," Yoram is obliged to correct Roger's pronunciation. As they take their seats, Roger reaches for the iced bowl of blini and caviar that has been set out on the conference room table along with a tray of Mai Tais (see Trader Vic's Mai Tai, page 14).

"Caviar and blinis; Mai Tais," says Roger. "We're thinking about a land of exotic luxury."

"We'd like to think that if Beirut is the Paris of the Middle East, Haifa could be the Rome," adds Nick, who explains that his cruise line is charting its most luxurious ship along "all the wondrous ports of the Israeli Riviera."

Blini, or thin pancakes, are more closely associated with Russia and the Baltic States than with Israel; *blini* is the Russian word for pancake, after all. But many Israelis, including many who first settled Israel, have their roots in that part of the world.

Russian blini are typically eaten with fish (smoked, pickled, or salted) or, as at the Sterling Cooper conference table, with that ultimate symbol of culinary luxury, caviar. As Alexandra Kropotkin, the author of *The Best of Russian Cooking* (1964) from which this recipe for blini and caviar is adapted, writes, "Many Russians drink straight vodka with blini pancakes." Now *that's* a recipe we *know* Roger would enjoy.

Blini and Caviar

ADAPTED FROM THE BEST OF RUSSIAN COOKING
BY ALEXANDRA KROPOTKIN (CHARLES SCRIBNER'S SONS, 1964)

½ cup sifted all-purpose flour

½ teaspoon baking powder

¾ cup milk

½ teaspoon sugar

3 tablespoons sour cream, plus additional for
*   topping blini*

1 egg

Butter for frying

Caviar for topping

1. In a large bowl, sift the flour and baking powder together. Add the milk, sugar, and sour cream. Beat the egg until frothy, add to the batter, and stir well. Let batter stand for 20 minutes.

2. Melt butter on a griddle or large skillet. Fry small (2–3 inch) pancakes in very hot butter. Drain on paper towels. Top each blini with additional sour cream and caviar before serving.

YIELD: APPROXIMATELY 16–20 BLINI

See color insert.

It's been said that anyone who claims to remember the 1960s obviously wasn't there. But no matter what your lifestyle—straight (in the '60s sense), Bohemian, or hippie—if you were alive in the 1960s, chances are you ate, and remember, California Dip.

This simple concoction reflects the '60s trend toward easy-to-prepare packaged foods. The essential ingredient was nothing more, or less, than a package of dried onion soup mix. Combined thoroughly with sour cream and chilled, it made for a delicious accompaniment to chips, crackers, or toast. The challenge was to find chips or crackers sturdy enough to stand up to a swipe through a bowl of this thick and creamy delight. Ridged potato chips were a perfect solution, and we recommend Utz brand potato chips (ridged or regular), a staple in the Draper household and a major account at Sterling Cooper, for an authentic *Mad Men* experience. Founded by Bill and Sallie Utz in 1921, Utz isn't nearly as big a company as Frito-Lay or Wise, but it's a leading regional brand in the mid-Atlantic and Northeast.

In one of the most unforgettable scenes in *Mad Men*, Utz's owner Hunt Schilling and his wife, the very heavy-set Edith, visit Sterling Cooper to watch acerbic comedian Jimmy Barrett film an Utz commercial ("Utz are better than nuts!"; season 2, episode 3; "The Benefactor.") (For the record, Utz was never owned by anyone named Schilling.)

When Jimmy sees the overweight Mrs. Schilling, he launches into a vicious rant about her weight, at one point comparing her to the ill-fated blimp *Hindenburg*. The misstep nearly costs Sterling Cooper the account, salvaged only thanks to a carefully staged apology over dinner at Lutèce delivered by Jimmy but arranged by Don Draper (see Lutèce Gambas au Beurre d'Escargot, page 179).

According to Jean Anderson, author of the *American Century Cook Book* (Clarkson Potter, 1997), the idea of mixing Lipton's Onion Soup Mix and sour cream came not from Lipton's, but from an anonymous California cook (hence the name, California Dip) in 1954, two years after the soup mix first appeared on supermarket shelves. "Word of the new dip spread through Los Angeles faster than a canyon fire," wrote Anderson, "newspapers printed the recipe, onion soup mixes sales soared, and Lipton executives, a continent away in New Jersey, were ecstatic. They tracked down the recipe, perfected it, and beginning

A PACKAGE OF UTZ POTATO CHIPS CIRCA 1960

in 1958, printed it on every box of Lipton Recipe Secrets Onion Soup Mix." The location of its invention was a fortunate one: California was the hip, trend-setting state in the 1960s—*the* place to be or to emulate—and "New Jersey Dip" would likely have been a huge market failure.

In "Red in the Face," Paul Kinsey and Ken Cosgrove cajole Pete Campbell into opening a box containing a duplicate wedding present he and Trudy have received, one that will take some effort to return. Inside the box is a garish ceramic serving piece that looks like two large lettuce leaves joined at the base, onto which is mounted a ceramic tomato with a removable top. Paul and Ken are astonished; they can't believe Pete and Trudy received two identical monstrosities.

"What is it?" asks Ken.

"You have your friends over. You put chips in the sides and dip in the middle."

"Dip?" says Ken incredulously.

"Yes," Pete explains. "We went to these people's house and they had one. It had sour cream with these little brown onions in it. It was *very* good."

"You'll have to give me that recipe sometime," counters Ken, though it's hard to tell if he's serious.

Well, here you go, Ken—just in case.

California Dip

FROM LIPTON ONION SOUP ADVERTISEMENT, NOVEMBER, 1962

1 *envelope onion soup mix*
2 *cups sour cream*

Place ingredients in a medium bowl, stir, and chill. Serve with potato chips.

YIELD: 2 CUPS

GRAND CENTRAL OYSTER BAR'S OYSTERS ROCKEFELLER

SEASON 1, EPISODE 7

"Red in the Face"

"He was a bold man who first ate an oyster," says Roger Sterling to Don Draper as they enjoy drinks—an Old Fashioned for Don, a martini for Roger (see Don's Old Fashioned and Roger's Martini, page 9)—and oysters at an eatery near their office one day in 1960. "Look at you, I had no idea you were such a fan of the mollusk."

"I'm acquiring a taste," replies Don. "It's like eating a mermaid."

The restaurant isn't identified, but a likely destination for ad men working on Madison Avenue would have been the cavernous Grand Central Oyster Bar. This Manhattan institution opened in 1913, one level down from the street in New York's famed Grand Central Station, which opened the same year. Harry Crane's officemate, Warren McKenna, tells him, "We're going to the Oyster Bar," in season 2, episode 3 ("The Benefactor"). Harry declines, mostly because he's preoccupied with opening Ken Cosgrove's paycheck, which has been delivered to him in error. He's not hungry after seeing that Kenny earns more than he does.

The Oyster Bar, whose soaring, scallop-shaped ceilings are today lined with lightbulbs, gives the impression of sitting inside an enormous, illuminated oyster shell. Passengers waiting to board the Twentieth Century Limited to Chicago or any other train would often dine in the Oyster Bar before beginning their journeys. But the Oyster Bar was, and remains, a destination in and of itself and attracted a storied clientele that included the financier and philanthropist James Buchanan Brady—better known as "Diamond Jim"—and his paramour, the actress Lillian Russell. Boxer "Gentleman Jim" Corbett, Al Jolson, and Florenz Ziegfeld, the Broadway impresario of *Ziegfeld Follies* fame also dined there. Presidents Woodrow Wilson, Franklin Delano Roosevelt, and John F. Kennedy were just a few of the chief executives who have indulged in the Oyster Bar's seafood delicacies.

We already know Roger is a huge fan of the mollusk; he has Oysters Rockefeller delivered by room service at the hotel where he and Joan Holloway have one of their many liaisons (season 1, episode 6; "Babylon"). Though he and Don are downing dozens of unadorned raw oysters in this episode, we're tipping our hat to Roger here with the Oyster Bar's famed Oysters Rockefeller recipe, which first appeared in *The Grand Central Oyster Bar & Restaurant Seafood Cookbook* (1977). This is the version of Oysters Rockefeller as it was made in the early 1960s, served right in the pan. The recipe has since been changed, according to owner and executive chef Sandy Ingber. Today, the Grand Central Oyster Bar serves Oysters Rockefeller in a bed of creamed spinach and glazed with hollandaise sauce, and the dish remains one of the Oyster Bar's bestsellers.

THE DINING ROOM OF THE GRAND CENTRAL OYSTER BAR TODAY

Oysters Rockefeller

ADAPTED FROM THE GRAND CENTRAL OYSTER BAR AND RESTAURANT SEAFOOD COOKBOOK *(CROWN, 1977)*
WITH THE ASSISTANCE OF THE GRAND CENTRAL OYSTER BAR, NEW YORK, NEW YORK

Rock salt
2 dozen large (or 3–4 dozen small) oysters,
*   opened and on the half shell*
4 medium shallots (about ¼ cup), minced
1 small stalk celery, minced
¼ cup fresh parsley, minced
¾ cup (1½ sticks) butter, softened and divided
2 cups fresh spinach, coarsely chopped
⅓ cup soft bread crumbs
1–2 drops Worcestershire sauce
½ teaspoon salt
Sprinkling of freshly ground black pepper
Pinch of cayenne pepper
2 tablespoons Pernod or Anisette

1. Preheat oven to 450°F. Fill 4 pie or cake tins (or a baking dish large enough to hold oysters) with rock salt, but no more than half full (use just enough salt to keep the oysters from rocking back and forth). Place the tins in the oven briefly to warm.

2. Prepare the topping: Sauté the shallots, celery, and parsley in 4 tablespoons of butter in a heavy skillet for approximately 5–7 minutes. Add spinach to the skillet and allow it to wilt for a minute.

3. Pour spinach mixture into a blender. Add the remaining butter, bread crumbs, Worcestershire sauce, salt, peppers, and Pernod or Anisette. Blend for a minute at medium speed.

Top each oyster with about 1 teaspoon to 1 tablespoon of the mixture, depending on the size of the oyster.

4. Remove the tins from the oven and embed the oysters firmly in the hot salt. Return pans to the oven and bake for about 4 minutes, or until the butter is melted and the spinach is lightly browned on top. Serve oysters right in the tin.

YIELD: 24 OYSTERS (ABOUT 4 SERVINGS)

See color insert.

FANS OF THE MOLLUSK

People have been eating oysters for millennia. Citizens of ancient Rome enjoyed them, as did the early Native Americans. And oysters are almost as varied as wine, with taste and texture determined by water conditions and geography. A Wellfleet oyster from Cape Cod isn't the same oyster that comes from the Gulf of Mexico near New Orleans, and neither of them is the same as an oyster from Washington State or the coast of Brittany. "Diamond Jim" Brady, who often visited the Oyster Bar two or three times a day, would bet the waiters he could tell a Wellfleet oyster from any other blindfolded. Though he never lost the bet, the $50 always turned into a tip.

Before overconsumption and pollution took their toll, the nineteenth-century waters around New York, including the bays of New York Harbor and Long Island Sound, produced some of the largest, sweetest oysters in the world and the oyster, according to William Grimes, author of *Appetite City: A Culinary History of New York* (Farrar, Straus and Giroux, 2009), was to New York what the lobster was to Boston and the crab to Baltimore. Oyster stands, oyster saloons (associated with vice and prostitution), and oyster cellars, literally basement establishments, dotted the city. (An oyster cellar existed in New York as early as 1763, on Broad Street.) "Today," writes Grimes, "only one restaurant in New York offers an approximation of the old oyster cellars: the Oyster Bar at Grand Central Terminal."

However, Oysters Rockefeller didn't originate in New York, as many assume. The original comes from one of New Orleans' most famous restaurants, Antoine's, and is based on a dish originally made with snails as early as 1850. Snails were no longer in favor by 1899, so Antoine's began serving the dish (which, much like the recipe included here, originally involved topping the seafood with greens, a butter sauce, and bread crumbs before baking or broiling) with Gulf oysters. Legend has it that a satisfied customer declared the dish "as rich as Rockefeller," referring to John D. Rockefeller, the nation's richest man. In truth, Jules Alciatore, the founder's son who was then the restaurant's owner, wanted a name that would suggest the dish was "the richest in the world," and Oysters Rockefeller was born. It's been a winner ever since, both at Antoine's and at the Grand Central Oyster Bar where Don falls in love with the mollusk.

JERRY'S DEVILED EGGS

SEASON 2, EPISODE 4

"Three Sundays"

As Peggy Olson and her extended family await the arrival of young parish priest Father John Gill for Sunday afternoon dinner, Jerry Respola, Peggy's brother-in-law, is lying on the living room couch nursing his (suspiciously) chronically bad back. On the coffee table in front of him is a plate of Deviled Eggs, often referred to as Stuffed Eggs in cookbooks of the period, and occasionally as Eggs Mimosa.

Two weeks later, on Easter Sunday, Peggy and Father Gill chat outside of church after Easter Services as young children hunt for colored Easter eggs. There is a hint of wistfulness in Peggy's expression, for she has given up for adoption the baby she conceived with Pete Campbell. As their conversation continues, Father Gill presses a blue Easter egg into her hand: "For the little one," he says. Does he mean Peggy's infant niece? Peggy appears to wonder if he knows her secret. In fact he does because Peggy's sister, Anita Olson Respola, ashamed of her sister's behavior, revealed it to Father Gill at confession.

The egg has great symbolic meaning in both Christianity and Judaism as a symbol of rebirth and renewal, and as an offering of kindness. It is, of course, also a ubiquitous symbol of fertility.

The notion of stuffing eggs originated, according to some sources, in ancient Rome, where it was common practice to pour spicy sauces over eggs. The earliest recipes for stuffed boiled eggs appear in medieval European texts, which include fillings of cheese, raisins, and spices. By the late 1500s and early 1600s, such stuffed eggs were widely consumed. The term *deviling*, which implies hot or spicy, is from the eighteenth century, though spicy stuffed eggs existed earlier.

Deviled eggs were extraordinarily popular in the 1950s and 1960s and could be found on party platters, at picnics, in lunch boxes, and on kitchen tables across America. It seemed almost every American cookbook of the period had a deviled egg recipe, and with good reason; people find them irresistible.

This recipe for Deviled Eggs is adapted from the very popular *All New Fannie Farmer Boston Cooking-School Cookbook* by Wilma Lord Perkins (1959). If you have a fertile imagination, however, you may wish to improvise and give birth to a new recipe you can call your own.

Deviled Eggs

ADAPTED FROM THE ALL NEW FANNIE FARMER BOSTON COOKING-SCHOOL
COOKBOOK *BY WILMA LORD PERKINS (LITTLE, BROWN, 1959)*

6 eggs, at room temperature
¼ cup mayonnaise, or more if you prefer a
  creamier filling
¼ teaspoon dry mustard, or more to taste
Dash of cayenne
Salt and ground black pepper
Paprika, for sprinkling

1. Hard boil the eggs: Bring a pot of water (with enough water to cover eggs) to a boil. Place eggs carefully in the pan. Reduce heat to a simmer and cook for 15–20 minutes. Place eggs immediately in cold water.

2. Make stuffing: Peel eggs and cut in half lengthwise. Carefully remove yolks and place in a small bowl. Set whites aside on a plate. Mash yolks until fine and crumbly (you can also press through a strainer to avoid lumps). Add mayonnaise and stir until mixture has a smooth consistency. Add mustard and cayenne pepper. Season to taste with salt and pepper.

3. Refill hollow in whites with yolk mixture. Sprinkle with paprika. Cover and refrigerate. Serve chilled.

YIELD: 12 EGG HALVES

SARDI'S STEAK TARTAR

SEASON 2, EPISODE 5

"The New Girl"

There's no eatery more emblematic of Broadway and the New York theater world than Sardi's on West 44th Street. An institution since 1921, this restaurant is a favorite of actors, playwrights, producers, and directors. Its famed walls are lined with framed caricatures of every big name, and a few lesser lights, whose talents have graced the Great White Way over the decades.

When actress Shirley Booth came to Sardi's after her debut in *Come Back, Little Sheba* in 1950, she inspired a spontaneous standing ovation. Thus began the tradition of opening night parties at Sardi's, a tradition that continues to this day.

"During a typical dinner at Sardi's you are likely to have canapés with Marlene Dietrich, soup with Ethel Merman, your meat served next to Rex Harrison and salad elbow-rubbed by Marilyn Monroe," wrote Broadway great Victor Borge in the foreword to *Curtain Up at Sardi's* (Random House, 1957), a cookbook co-authored by Vincent Sardi, Jr. (the son of the founder) and Helen Bryson. "East or west of the Hudson River, Sardi's is always the most interesting place in Manhattan, Monday's through Sardi's!"

SARDI'S ON WEST 44TH STREET IN 1965

When Bobbi Barrett, the wife and tough-minded business manager of comedian Jimmy Barrett, sells a pilot of a TV show starring her husband, she calls Don Draper to join her for a celebratory dinner. Jimmy happens to be pitchman for Sterling Cooper client Utz Potato Chips, and Bobbi and Don have recently started an affair.

"Where are you?" asks Don.

"I'm at Sardi's, surrounded by clowns," she replies, though the one clown missing in action this evening is her husband.

The lights are low as Don joins Bobbi at her table. She's already sipping a martini and, knowing Don's drink of choice, bids the waiter to bring him an Old Fashioned. When she says to Don, "So, what do I want?" he doesn't hesitate: steak tartare. This Sardi's classic has been around since at least the 1940s, and is still prepared tableside today just as it was half a century ago. Sardi's graciously provided its original steak tartare recipe expressly for *The Unofficial Mad Men Cookbook*.

Tableside preparation was, and remains, a sign of class, elegance, and French-inspired sophistication. The servers at today's Sardi's will prepare the ground beef concoction with your choice of anchovies, pasteurized eggs, capers, and chopped onions for $29.50, about half a week's wage for the typical Sterling Cooper copywriter back in 1961.

Steak Tartar

COURTESY OF SARDI'S RESTAURANT, NEW YORK, NEW YORK

NOTE: All ingredients should be cold before you begin.

2 tablespoons capers
2 tablespoons red onions, finely chopped
1½ tablespoons anchovy paste
1 tablespoon English mustard
1 teaspoon pasteurized egg yolk
Fresh cracked black pepper, to taste
1 teaspoon olive oil
5 dashes Tabasco Sauce (mild)
2½ tablespoons Worcestershire sauce
8 ounces steak (5 ounces sirloin steak and 3
*   ounces filet mignon, finely ground)*
Salt, to taste
2 slices black bread, toasted (optional)
1 tablespoon egg yolk from a hard-boiled egg
*   (finely chopped), for garnish*

1. Stir together capers, red onions, anchovy paste, English mustard, pasteurized egg yolk, black pepper, and olive oil in a medium bowl until semi-paste-like. Add Tabasco and Worcestershire sauces and mix until evenly blended with a wooden spoon. Mix in the beef and add salt to taste and mix until well blended.

2. Roll the tartare in the bowl with a spoon. Place on a serving plate, and flatten with spoon and form into an elongated oval shape. With a knife, score in a criss-cross shape. Serve on a cold plate with toasted black bread, and garnish with finely chopped egg yolk.

YIELD: 1 SERVING

TRADER VIC'S AMERICANIZED VERSION OF POLYNESIAN CUISINE HELPED FUEL
INTEREST IN FOREIGN FARE IN THE MID-TWENTIETH CENTURY

BETTY'S AROUND THE WORLD DINNER: GAZPACHO AND RUMAKI

SEASON 2, EPISODE 8
"A Night to Remember"

At a dinner party hosted by Don and Betty Draper for Roger and Mona Sterling, Herman "Duck" Phillips, public relations executive Crab Colson, and Crab's wife Peta, Betty unwittingly proves Don right about the market niche their client, Heineken Beer, should pursue. Days before the dinner, Duck asserts that Heineken wants to "compete at the tap" for the predominantly male market that drinks outside the home. Don sees a different, largely untapped market in affluent housewives, like Betty, who want to play the sophisticated, worldly hostess.

"For women entertaining in the home," argued Don, "Holland is Paris. They can buy this sophisticated beer and proudly walk it into the kitchen instead of hiding it in the garage."

The early 1960s was a time of transition in American culinary tastes. The American meat and potatoes dinner was yielding to inspiration from abroad, thanks to a curiosity about more exotic fare inspired by chefs such as Julia Child. This was especially true in the homes of those who aspired to affect a more refined, cultured persona (see page 162).

When the Drapers and their guests assemble around the dining room table, Betty tells them the night's dinner is going to take them around the world. There's gazpacho from Spain, rumaki from Japan (typically chicken livers and water chestnut wrapped in bacon with a soy marinade), lamb from nearby Dutchess County, New York, and egg noodles from Germany, just like her grandmother used to make. She then motions to the buffet and offers wine from France and frosted bottles of Heineken Beer from Holland.

Duck voices his suspicion that Don put her up to buying Heineken to prove his point, but Betty is obviously not in on the joke. Don's point is made and his reputation for uncanny advertising savvy is proven yet again.

Because they can be paired successfully with virtually any main course, gazpacho and rumaki were exceptionally popular starters in the 1960s. We selected these two features of Betty's Around the World Dinner for your enjoyment.

GAZPACHO

This chilled soup of Spanish origin is as close as you can come to sipping a salad. There are countless interpretations of gazpacho, but the most commonly used ingredients are tomatoes, peppers, onions, cucumber, garlic, olive oil, vinegar, and bread crumbs. Gazpacho is a refreshing way to start a meal, especially in the warm-weather months, or it can be eaten alone for lunch or dinner. So emblematic of Spain is gazpacho that Don or Betty would have found it served at the Spanish pavilion had they ventured to the New York World's Fair in 1964.

Though the dish has its roots in Spain, the word *gazpacho* is Arabic in origin and means "soaked bread," according to *Larousse Gastronomique* (Clarkson Potter, 2001). The Moors brought their culinary influence with them when they invaded Andalusia from North Africa in the Middle Ages, and this included early gazpacho-type recipes that had the characteristics of soup and salad even though tomatoes, a fruit native to the Americas, were unknown to them.

Spanish/Mediterranean dishes such as paella, sangria, and gazpacho were among the international foods gaining popularity in the 1950s and 1960s. Simple to prepare, especially with modern appliances such as the blender and food processor, gazpacho was as close as you can get to a hit every time. As Betty clearly knew, it was the perfect way to begin your own Around the World Dinner.

Gazpacho

ADAPTED FROM THE BETTER HOMES AND GARDENS NEW COOKBOOK *(MEREDITH, 1962)*

1 cup finely chopped peeled tomato

½ cup chopped green pepper

½ cup finely chopped celery

½ cup finely chopped cucumber

¼ cup chopped onion

2 teaspoons snipped parsley

1 teaspoon snipped chives

1 small clove garlic, minced

2–3 tablespoons wine vinegar

2 tablespoons olive oil

1 teaspoon salt

¼ teaspoon fresh ground black pepper

Dash of cayenne pepper

½ teaspoon Worcestershire sauce

2 cups tomato juice

Caesar Croutons, for serving (see Caesar Croutons, page 148)

1. Combine all ingredients except croutons in stainless steel or glass bowl. Cover and chill thoroughly, at least 4 hours.

2. Serve in chilled cups. Top with croutons.

YIELD: 6 SERVINGS

See color insert.

RUMAKI

Though Betty told her guests that rumaki is from Japan, its origins are murky. The word *rumaki* may derive from the Japanese word *harumaki*, or spring roll, but its heritage remains ambiguous. Some say this rich appetizer has Polynesian roots, while others insist it was invented by restaurateur Victor Bergeron—better known as Trader Vic—the man behind the California-based chain of popular Polynesian-themed restaurants. Still others attribute rumaki to Trader Vic's major competitor, Don the Beachcomber, the restaurateur considered the father of the tiki bar and restaurant. Don's décor and cuisine (strong, rum-based cocktails and Chinese-based food) were loosely inspired by primitive Polynesian tribes. Rumaki appeared on the menu of the Don the Beachcomber Restaurant in Palm Springs as early as 1941. (For more on Trader Vic's and Don the Beachcomber, see Trader Vic's Mai Tai, page 14.)

Regardless of who invented it, rumaki enjoyed exceptional popularity for decades. In 1958, the legendary food writer Clementine Paddleford (see Palm Springs Chile Rellenos, page 98) lauded the rumaki served at the Hotel Lexington's Hawaiian Room in New York. Rumaki was still going strong more than a decade later when, in 1970, newspaper columnist Amy Vanderbilt declared rumaki "a great specialty of the Trader Vic's restaurants where I always order it."

Rumaki isn't in fashion as it once was, but your guests, like Betty's, are in for a flavorful treat.

Rumaki

ADAPTED FROM THE NEW YORK TIMES COOKBOOK *BY CRAIG CLAIBORNE (HARPER & ROW, 1961)*

6 chicken livers, cut into 1-inch pieces

18 canned water chestnuts, sliced

9 bacon slices, cut into thirds

9 scallions, sliced thin lengthwise and cut into 1-inch pieces

½ cup soy sauce

¼ teaspoon ground ginger

½ teaspoon curry powder

1. Slice the chicken livers into 3 pieces and fold each piece over a water chestnut slice.

2. Wrap a strip of bacon and scallion around the liver/chestnut core, pinning each kabob with 2 toothpicks.

3. Combine soy sauce, ginger, and curry powder in a small bowl. Place kabobs in baking dish and cover with soy sauce mixture. Place in refrigerator, and marinate the kabobs for 1 hour.

4. Remove kabobs from refrigerator. Drain marinade. Broil kabobs in a preheated broiler, turning frequently until bacon is thoroughly cooked, about 5 minutes. Serve on wood skewers.

YIELD: 8–12 SERVINGS

PALM SPRINGS CHILE RELLENOS

SEASON 2, EPISODE 11

"The Jet Set"

In 1948, a forty-nine year old "roving food editor" for *This Week* magazine (and later a food writer for, among other publications, the *New York Herald Tribune*) commenced a twelve-year, 800,000-mile odyssey to virtually every corner of the United States to learn about the culinary habits of Americans. That journey resulted in the publication of Clementine Paddleford's *How America Eats* (1960), a collection of recipes drawn from every region of the country.

"How does America eat?" asked Paddleford in the book's foreword. "She eats on the fat of the land. She eats in every language. For the most part, however, even with the increasingly popular trend toward foreign foods, the dishes come to the table with an American accent."

When Don Draper travels to Los Angeles to drum up business for Sterling Cooper at a convention of aerospace manufacturers, he meets Joy, a beautiful ingénue who urges him to come with her to Palm Springs.

"I don't know about that," says Don.

"Why would you deny yourself something you want?" she replies suggestively.

As she gets into her white Mercedes convertible, Don impulsively joins her. He doesn't need to bring his luggage; it's been lost by TWA anyway. Without a word to Pete Campbell, who has also made the trip west, Don and Joy roar off into the sunshine, leaving Pete to fend for himself.

In Palm Springs, Joy tells Don they'll be having dinner soon.

"Have you ever had Mexican food?" asks Joy.

"No," Don replies.

Indeed, Mexican food would have been hard for Don to find in New York in the early 1960s, but not unheard of. Mexican cuisine came to the United States with the large influx of Mexican immigrants to California in the 1950s. Mexican restaurants began popping up throughout the Golden State in the early '60s, including Palm Springs. El Parador Café, founded in 1959, claims to be the first Mexican restaurant in New York City, but the cuisine had yet to become as popular as it was in trendy California.

"You're going to like it," Joy assures him.

That evening, at the spectacular desert home Joy and a group of European friends are enjoying courtesy of wealthy friends traveling in Sardinia, they enjoy a Mexican dinner prepared by the house staff. Their sumptuous meal includes a pepper filled with cheese and a sauce, known as chile rellenos. This dish typically consists of poblano peppers stuffed with cheese (though meat is also sometimes used), then covered in egg batter and fried. Chile rellenos have been part of the cuisine in Mexico for hundreds of years, but in 1962 were an exotic new taste for a New Yorker like Don. This chile rellenos recipe celebrating Don's trip to California is adapted from Clementine Paddleford's *How America Eats*.

Chile Rellenos

FROM HOW AMERICA EATS *BY CLEMENTINE PADDLEFORD*
(CHARLES SCRIBNER'S SONS, 1960)

For the sauce

*1 (15-ounce) can crushed or diced tomatoes,
with juice*
½ cup minced onion
Salt and ground black pepper

For the chiles

*2 cans whole green chiles (already roasted and
peeled, about 3 chiles per can)*
3–4 ounces Jack or Cheddar cheese, sliced
3 eggs, separated
1 tablespoon canola oil

1. Make the sauce: Combine tomatoes, juice, onion, and salt and pepper to taste. Cook over low heat until onions are tender, about 15 minutes. Let gently simmer while making chiles.

2. Make the chiles: Split and remove any seeds from chile peppers. Place a thin strip of cheese in each cavity and fold chile over cheese.

3. Beat egg yolks until fluffy. Beat egg whites until stiff but not dry. Fold whites into yolks.

4. Dip the chiles into the egg mixture, coating as well as possible. Pick the chiles out with a spoon, along with a bit of the mixture.

5. Heat oil in a medium skillet. Gently sauté chiles over medium heat until the underside is brown. Use a spatula to turn each chile quickly (each chile looks like an individual omelet). Brown on each side until done. Place the "omelets" on a plate, and place a dollop of sauce on top of each omelet.

YIELD: 4 APPETIZER SERVINGS

ROCKEFELLER FUNDRAISER HORS D'OEUVRES

SEASON 3, EPISODE 9

"Wee Small Hours"

A debonair gentleman approaches a very pregnant Betty Draper outside the ladies' room at the Long Island country club where Jane and Roger Sterling are hosting their Kentucky Derby–themed garden party (season 3, episode 3; "My Old Kentucky Home").

"I wish you were waiting for me," he says, as smooth an opening line as we've ever heard. After asking her what it feels like to be pregnant, he makes a startlingly intimate gesture: "I'm going to blame this on martinis," he says, "but may I?" He extends his hand, Betty nods, and Henry Francis touches Betty—who will soon become Mrs. Henry Francis—for the first time. But it's not until later in the evening that they meet formally: Bert Cooper introduces Betty and Don to Henry and we learn Henry works as an aide to New York governor Nelson Rockefeller. He has come to the party directly from Rockefeller's wedding.

Betty next meets Henry when she seeks his help on behalf of the Junior League of Tarrytown. The mutual attraction is clear, and Betty begins looking for ways to stay in touch.

One morning, Betty reads a headline in the *New York Times* proclaiming that GOP experts are writing off Rockefeller's chances for the 1964 presidential nomination. This prompts Betty to mail Henry a note that ends: "Does anyone else read this?" He replies a few days later, "Dear Betty…not anymore. H."

When Henry appears at Betty's house unannounced in the middle of the day, she is nonplussed. They share a moment, but only until Carla, the housekeeper, comes in. To mask the nature of his visit, Henry tells Betty her home looks like a perfect venue for a fundraiser and leaves quickly, but Carla's face betrays her suspicion.

To cover her tracks, Betty places a businesslike call to Henry, while Don sits nearby, to tell him they can host the fundraiser. Henry is puzzled; for a moment he doesn't recall his off-the-cuff remark that morning. But now the event is on. When the day arrives, Betty feels betrayed when Henry sends an aide in his stead.

The Rockefeller fundraiser as depicted in *Mad Men* was a typical 1960s-style cocktail party. About a dozen men and women, formally dressed, sip cocktails and nibble on finger foods: canapés, shrimp, and dips. These "nibblers," as some called them, are, in the words of the *New Good Housekeeping Cookbook* (Harcourt, Brace & World, 1963), "tantalizing little party foods."

In creating our own cocktail party hors d'oeuvres menu, we drew inspiration from Betty's and culled dozens of cookbooks to arrive at an appetizer selection representative of the era and the setting. We chose several that Henry Francis would have regretted missing.

CANAPÉS

See color insert.

These miniature toasts were a fixture of the cocktail party scene in the 1950s and '60s. Virtually every cookbook of the era offered canapé recipes with toppings ranging from caviar, hot cheddar cheese, and deviled chicken to liverwurst, lobster, and toasted Parmesan. Easy to make and easy to eat while managing a cocktail with the other hand, the canapé boasted virtually endless permutations. Taste and texture will vary depending on the base (we use Melba toasts) and the toppings. Ours include toppings of mushroom, a Parmesan onion mix, curry butter with shrimp, and cream cheese chutney spreads.

Canapés are also easy to serve. As Joan Holloway says to Roger Sterling about the way Shirley MacLaine's character, Fran Kubelik, was mistreated in the 1960 film, *The Apartment*, "The way those men treated that poor girl, handing her around like a tray of canapés?" (season 1, episode 10; "Long Weekend"). It's no way to treat a woman, but canapés are meant to be passed around…on a tray.

Chutney Canapé Spread

ADAPTED FROM JAMES BEARD'S HORS D'OEUVRES
AND CANAPÉS BY JAMES BEARD (WILLIAM MORROW & CO., 1963)

3 *tablespoons prepared mango chutney*

2 *tablespoons chopped preserved ginger*

2 *tablespoons grated fresh coconut*
   (or sweetened coconut flakes)

2 *teaspoons curry powder*

8 *ounces cream cheese*

2 *tablespoons chopped blanched almonds*
   (optional)

40 *Melba Toast rounds (see Melba Toast, page 108)*

Place ingredients in a small bowl, mix well, and spread on
Melba Toast rounds.

YIELD: 40 CANAPÉS

Shrimp Curry Butter Canapés

ADAPTED FROM THE PLAYBOY GOURMET BY THOMAS MARIO (CROWN, 1961)

*1 pound small–medium shrimp, peeled
(approximately 30 shrimp)*
Salt, for water and for sprinkling
2 teaspoons lemon juice
½ cup (1 stick) butter, softened
2 teaspoons curry powder
½ teaspoon ground coriander
30 Melba toast rounds (see Melba Toast, page 108)
Ground white pepper, for sprinkling
2 finely chopped chives, for sprinkling

1. Boil 2 cups water; add shrimp, salt, and lemon juice. Cook covered for 3–5 minutes, until shrimp are pink and cooked through. Drain and chill.

2. In a small mixing bowl, combine butter, curry powder, and coriander. Blend well; spread butter on toast and top with a shrimp. Sprinkle with salt, white pepper, and chopped chives.

YIELD: 30 CANAPÉS

Mushroom Canapés

ADAPTED FROM BETTY CROCKER'S NEW GOOD AND EASY COOKBOOK *(GOLDEN PRESS, 1962)*

1 pound mushrooms, finely chopped

2 tablespoons butter

1 teaspoon Worcestershire sauce

Salt, to taste

½ teaspoon onion salt

¼ cup grated Parmesan cheese

20 Melba toast rounds (see Melba Toast, page 108)

Minced parsley, for garnish

1. Make mushroom spread: Sauté chopped mushrooms in butter. Season with Worcestershire sauce, salt, and onion salt. Remove from heat and stir in Parmesan cheese.

2. Mound mixture on Melba Toast rounds and heat under broiler until bubbling. Garnish with parsley before serving.

YIELD: 20 CANAPÉS

Toasted Parmesan Canapés

ADAPTED FROM LADIES' HOME JOURNAL COOKBOOK,
BY CAROL TRUAX, ED. (DOUBLEDAY, 1963)

¾ cup minced onion
½ cup mayonnaise
⅓ cup Parmesan cheese, plus extra for sprinkling
20 Melba Toast rounds (see Melba Toast, page 108)
Paprika, for sprinkling

1. Mix onion, mayonnaise, and Parmesan cheese in a small bowl. Spread on toast pieces. Sprinkle extra Parmesan cheese, and then sprinkle with paprika.

2. Before serving, broil 3 inches from heat for 2–3 minutes, or until golden brown.

YIELD: 20 CANAPÉS

Homemade Melba Toast

FROM JULIA CHILD & COMPANY *BY JULIA CHILD (KNOPF, 1978)*

NOTE: Melba toast is a thin, dry toast that makes a wonderful base for canapés. James Beard and other chefs regularly called for them in canapé recipes of the 1960s. We like using Julia Child's recipe as a base for our canapé toppings.

We prefer to use thinly sliced sandwich bread, such as Pepperidge Farm, but the original recipe calls for a nonsweet sandwich loaf, at least a day old.

The toasts may be prepared well in advance, refrigerated or frozen, and recrisped in the oven before serving.

1 *loaf sandwich bread (see note above)*

1. Preheat oven to 275°F. If using an unsliced loaf of bread, cut into very thin slices approximately 1/16-inch thick. Trim crust and cut the bread diagonally into triangles, or use a cutter to make circles or your desired shapes.

2. Arrange in one layer, preferably on one or two cookie sheets, and bake slowly in the upper- and/or lower-middle levels until the bread has dried out and is starting to color. Remove from oven and cool on a rack.

YIELD: APPROXIMATELY 60 MELBA TOASTS

CHEESEBALLS

Another mid-century classic was the cheeseball: a mixture of cheeses processed until creamy, spiced with accents such as Worcestershire sauce, garlic, and hot pepper sauce, formed into a ball, and rolled, typically in spices and nuts. For convenience and presentation we chose a recipe for mini-cheeseballs.

Cream Cheese and Nut Balls

FROM THE VOGUE BOOK OF MENUS AND RECIPES
BY JESSICA DAVES (HARPER & ROW, 1964)

8 ounces salted almonds
8 ounces cream cheese
½ cup grated Parmesan cheese
2 dashes Tabasco
Crackers, for serving

1. Grind almonds in a grinder or food processor. Mix crushed almonds with cheeses and Tabasco until all are smoothly mixed.

2. Chill thoroughly, then mold into balls about ½ inch in diameter. Chill again before serving. Serve with crackers.

YIELD: 36–40 BALLS

COCKTAIL NIBBLERS (CHEX MIX)

NIBBLERS' DELIGHT!

PARTY MIX

FOR EASY, ECONOMICAL ENTERTAINING

Made in Minutes With Bite Size

RICE CHEX and **WHEAT CHEX**

RECIPE ON OTHER SIDE

AT PARTIES AND IN FRONT OF THE TELEVISION SET, CHEX MIX
WAS A UBIQUITOUS SNACK OF THE 1950S AND '60S

This mix, which uses Chex brand cereal as a base, has been a popular cocktail party nosh for more than half a century. Typically combined with pretzels, nuts, and seasoning and served toasted or warm, the salty Chex Mix will ensure your guests don't ignore the cocktails. Ralston Purina introduced Chex in 1942, and recipes for the mix began appearing on Chex boxes a decade later. As television became a part of daily American life, snack foods designed for watching "the tube" proliferated. Dubbed a "TV mix," you ate it with bowl in one hand and eyes glued to the television. Regardless, it works just as well as a cocktail party nibbler. The seasoning in *McCall's Cook Book* (1963) differs slightly from the official Chex party mix, but it's a winner.

Cocktail Nibblers

ADAPTED FROM THE MCCALL'S COOK BOOK BY THE
FOOD EDITORS OF MCCALL'S (RANDOM HOUSE, 1963)

2 cups pretzel sticks

¾ cup peanuts

6 cups rice, corn, and/or wheat crispy cereal
     squares, such as Chex

4 teaspoons Worcestershire sauce

¼ teaspoon garlic salt

¼ teaspoon onion salt

¼ teaspoon celery salt

6 tablespoons butter, melted

1. Preheat oven to 250°F. Break pretzels into small pieces. Mix with peanuts and cereals on a large roasting pan.

2. Add Worcestershire sauce, garlic salt, onion salt, and celery salt to butter. Pour over mixture and combine thoroughly. Bake for about 1 hour, stirring every 15 minutes.

YIELD: APPROXIMATELY 8 CUPS MIX

DIP

You need a dip to add zest to crackers and chips. Dips made with Lipton's Onion Soup Mix, like Pete's California Dip (see page 79), were ubiquitous in the Draper era. We recommend that one and offer another: an avocado "dunk." How avocados became popular with American consumers is a tale an ad man like Don would surely appreciate. When Americans were slow to take to the fruit in the early twentieth century, an ad man suggested a representative of the avocado growers' association deny vehemently the "rumor" that avocados were an aphrodisiac. The result was predictable.

Avocado Dunk

FROM LIFE'S PICTURE COOK BOOK *(TIME, 1958)*

2 avocados
¼ cup mayonnaise
2 tablespoons lemon juice
1 teaspoon chili powder
1 garlic clove, mashed
Freshly ground black pepper
Corn chips, for serving

1. Peel avocados and mash the pulp with a fork. Add other ingredients and mix well.

2. Cover and let stand for at least 1 hour. Serve with corn chips.

YIELD: ABOUT 2 CUPS

THE HOSTESS WITH THE MOSTEST

Tips for a Successful Mad Men–Style Cocktail Party

Cookbooks, etiquette books, and magazines from the 1950s and '60s were filled with tips on entertaining, and advice on everything from how to fold the napkins to how to choose compatible guests. We culled a pile of '60s books and magazines for this list of helpful hints for *Mad Men*–style entertaining. The words *appetizers*, *nibblers*, and *hors d'oeuvres* are used interchangeably.

Cocktails

- Don't offer more than three types of mixed drinks, unless you hire a professional bartender. Have nonalcoholic alternatives available for those not indulging.

- Your well-stocked liquor cabinet should contain bourbon, blended whiskey, Scotch whiskey, and Canadian whiskey (for more on these whiskey varieties, see Canadian Clubhouse Punch and Lucky Strike Holiday Eggnog, page 54), gin, rum, vodka, dry and sweet vermouth, brandy, and various liqueurs. Remember, many cocktails also include nonalcoholic ingredients such as fruit, fruit juices, and soda water, so be sure your shopping list includes these extras once you have the evening's cocktail menu set.

- The host should abstain from drinking, or at least remain "fairly sober." And don't ply your guests with drinks, either. A host, according to Thomas Mario, author of *Playboy's Host & Bar Book* (Playboy Press, 1971), must remember that he or she is "a host and not a hustler."

- The cocktail hour should be limited to one hour if dinner is being served, even if guests are late.

- Harmonize the appetizers and the cocktails. If you're serving guacamole and chips, for example, tequila- and rum-based cocktails are in order; if Italian meats are served, Campari and soda is a nice complement.

Food

- If you're trying out a new dish or cocktail, give it a test run before you serve it to guests. As noted chef James Beard once wrote, "If you are fond of your friends, don't make guinea pigs of them."

- Show some imagination. Peanuts from a can and potato chips from a bag do not a cocktail party make, even with killer cocktails.

- If dinner is to follow, plan your hors d'oeuvres with that in mind. If the dinner is rich, keep the hors d'oeuvres light; if the dinner is light, go richer and more plentiful on the hors d'oeuvres. Avoid serving foods featured in your main course as hors d'oeuvres.

- Serve fewer types of nibblers, but more of each type.

- Pass the hors d'oeuvres twice, then let guests help themselves. Trays may be set wherever they will be easily accessible to guests.

- If serving canapés (see Rockefeller Fundraiser Hors d'Oeuvres, page 102), keep them small; a canapé should last no more than three bites. Plan on about four canapés per guest. No canapé should have a disposable part, such as an olive pit or shrimp tail.

- Avoid dishes that call for split-second timing, such as soufflés, to reduce stress and culinary calamities.

- Avoid creating a smoky house by not using the broiler or stovetop while you entertain.

Social

- Don't invite more people than your entertaining space can comfortably hold.

- Choose you guests wisely. How you mix your guests can be as important as how you mix your drinks. As James Beard wrote, "Remember the Montagues and the Capulets and plan accordingly."

- Greet every guest at the door.

- Never urge food on anyone. If a guest declines, accept without comment.

EGG ROLLS STERLING COOPER STYLE

French and Mexican foods, along with other foreign fare, first gained widespread popularity in the 1960s, but Americans were already quite familiar with two other foreign cuisines: Italian and Chinese, particularly the Cantonese style. Chinese immigrants in San Francisco and New York opened restaurants before the turn of the twentieth century. According to Andrew Coe, author of *Chop Suey: A Cultural History of Chinese Food in America* (Oxford, 2009), by mid century you could probably find such mainstays as chop suey, chow mein, egg rolls, and egg foo young at restaurants even in Omaha.

After World War II, Chinese restaurateurs followed their customers from the city to the suburbs and competed with fast-food restaurants and pizza joints to serve large meals at small prices. This wasn't fine dining, but for those who grew up in the postwar period of the 1950s and '60s it was exotic enough and easy to find. While the first Mexican restaurant didn't open in New York City until 1959 (see Palm Springs Chile Rellenos, page 98), by 1958 there were 110 Chinese restaurants in Washington, D.C., and likely more in New York. Two successful American restaurateurs, Victor Bergeron of Trader Vic's fame and Ernest Gantt, known as Don the Beachcomber, also popularized Chinese food, served with a Polynesian flair, at their national chains (see Trader Vic's Mai Tai, page 14, and Betty's Around the World Dinner: Gazpacho and Rumaki, page 93).

Chinese food had a practical appeal, too, because it could very conveniently be boxed up for consumption elsewhere. Save for the temperature, it looked and tasted the same, some would argue even better, after two hours in a little white box as it did when it was prepared. "Take-out" boxes with Chinese leftovers could be found in many an office refrigerator, including Sterling Cooper's.

Which brings us to an American creation inspired by the lighter Asian spring roll: the humble, yet ever-satisfying, egg roll. In 1963, *New York Times* food writer Craig Claiborne described the egg roll as "coming into its own as a popular snack" all over New York City, though it is often served as an appetizer. Egg rolls are a mixture of cooked vegetables (typically bean sprouts, celery, and/or cabbage), meat (usually pork, shrimp, and/or chicken), and seasonings rolled in a dough and pan or deep-fried. Crunchy on the outside and soft on the inside, eggs rolls are typically dipped in duck sauce or spicy mustard.

Egg rolls make several appearances in *Mad Men*, first when Rachel Menken and a friend discuss Rachel's attraction to Don Draper over lunch at an upscale Chinese restaurant (season 1, episode 11; "Indian Summer"). Egg rolls are part of an office buffet at Sterling Cooper (season 2, episode 4; "Three Sundays"), and Joan Holloway and Greg Harris' Chinese take-out (season 2, episode 8; "A Night to Remember"). A plate piled high with perfectly formed, crispy egg rolls is also part of the Christmas cheer when Sterling Cooper Draper Pryce throws a holiday party in honor of Lee Garner, Jr., of Lucky Strike (season 4, episode 2; "Christmas Comes But Once a Year").

This egg roll recipe is adapted from *How to Cook and Eat in Chinese* by Buwei Yang Chao (1963). A Japanese-trained physician, Chao settled in Cambridge, Massachusetts, with her Harvard professor husband and set out, according to Andrew Coe, "to do far more than publish recipes of her favorite dishes. Her goal was recreating the traditional Chinese way of eating on United States soil." Famed author Pearl S. Buck wrote the preface to Chao's cookbook and was extravagant in her praise. "I would like to nominate her for the Nobel Peace Prize," wrote Buck of Chao. "For what better road to universal peace is there than to gather around the table where new and delicious dishes are set forth which, though untasted by us, we are destined to enjoy and love? What better road to friendship, upon which alone peace can stand? I consider this cookbook a contribution to international understanding." We can't make such lofty claims for the egg roll, but when we tasted these we wanted to throw a party for Lee Garner, Jr., ourselves.

Egg Rolls

ADAPTED FROM HOW TO COOK AND EAT IN CHINESE
BY BUWEI YANG CHAO (RANDOM HOUSE, 1963)

NOTE: Shredded beef may be used in place of shredded pork.
Egg rolls can be cut into shorter sections before serving, if desired.
Assemble egg rolls just before cooking.

2 tablespoons soy sauce
2 tablespoons sherry
1½ teaspoons cornstarch
1 teaspoon sugar
1 teaspoon salt
3 tablespoons canola oil
1 pound pork, shredded
½ pound fresh shrimp, chopped
1 medium carrot, shredded
¼ pound mushrooms, diced
3 scallions, thinly sliced
1 pound bean sprouts, rinsed and dried
16 eggroll wrappers
Enough vegetable oil for deep-frying
Apricot Sauce (see recipe, page 118), for serving

1. Combine soy sauce, sherry, cornstarch, sugar, and salt in a
   small bowl.

2. Heat the oil in a skillet over high heat. Add the shredded
   pork and shrimp and cook for 1 minute. Remove pork and
   shrimp and drain liquid. Set aside. Add carrot and mushrooms and stir-fry for several minutes. Add scallions and
   bean sprouts and stir for 2 more minutes;

return shrimp and pork to the skillet. Add soy sauce mixture and stir for the last 30 seconds. Remove from heat.

3. Place an egg roll wrapper with one corner pointing toward you. Place 2–3 tablespoons of filling on a wrapper and fold the bottom corner of the wrapper up to the center. Brush the unrolled edges with water. Fold the left and right corners to the center, squeeze gently and then roll up all the way. Repeat with remaining filling and wrappers.

4. Heat the oil for deep-frying over medium heat (lower heat if it has a tendency to smoke). Deep-fry the rolls for 6 minutes. Turn each side so it gets immersed, since the upper side tends to float outside of the oil. The rolls are done when they are golden brown. Drain on paper towels and serve immediately, or keep warm in the oven before serving. Serve with Apricot Sauce.

YIELD: 16 SERVINGS

APRICOT SAUCE

FROM PILLSBURY'S BEST OF THE BAKE-OFF COLLECTION *(CONSOLIDATED BOOK PUBLISHERS, 1959), RECIPE SUBMITTED BY SENIOR WINNER, MRS. ROBERT BATCHELOR, DEFIANCE OHIO*

> *2 cups apricot preserves*
> *¼ cup finely chopped pimiento*
> *2 tablespoons vinegar*

Place ingredients in a small saucepan, and bring to a boil. Simmer for 2 minutes, stirring occasionally.

YIELD: ABOUT 2 CUPS

THE FORUM OF THE TWELVE CAESARS'
GOLDEN EGGS OF CRASSUS AND MARINATED OLIVES
SEASON 4, EPISODE 7
"The Suitcase"

Peggy Olson started her career at Sterling Cooper as Don Draper's secretary, but she quickly proved herself to be creative and ambitious. She's promoted to copywriter and by the time Don, Bert Cooper, Roger Sterling, and Lane Pryce start their new firm, she's Don's top creative assistant.

For her birthday in May 1965, Peggy's boyfriend, the nerdy Mark Kerney, tells her he's taking her to the Forum of the Twelve Caesars, one of New York's most over-the-top concept restaurants. What he doesn't tell her is that he has invited Peggy's mother Katherine, her sister Anita Olson Respola, her brother-in-law Jerry Respola, and her roommate Veronika to join them. That night, as Peggy is about to leave, Don insists Peggy work late on an ad campaign he's not yet satisfied with. Having reached a nadir in his personal life, he's impatient, irritable, and desperate for company. He's also mildly inebriated. Peggy calls the restaurant and we see a waiter bring a phone to the table. She'll only be fifteen minutes, she tells Mark, but she never makes it.

The Forum of the Twelve Caesars was the brainchild of Joseph Baum, a hotel and restaurant man, who helped turn Restaurant Associates from a purveyor of coffee, beef stew, doughnuts, and pies into a major force in New York's fine dining scene. "Baum developed some highly unusual ideas about restaurants and how to make them appealing," wrote William Grimes, a former *New York Times* restaurant critic, in *Appetite City: A Culinary History of New York* (North Point Press, 2009). "His philosophy was a blend of showmanship and mysticism, backed up by intensive research, endless attention to detail, and exhaustive recipe testing."

Restaurant Associates was looking to open a new restaurant in a Rockefeller Center location in 1956. Rockefeller Center, writes Grimes, was "a crossroads where the radio and television industries met advertising and publishing" and "suggested to Baum...the idea of a forum." Serendipitously, one of Baum's designers had recently purchased a set of large portraits of the twelve Caesars—Julius and the first eleven emperors of Rome—and the Forum of the Twelve Caesars, one of the most extravagant restaurants ever to grace New York City, came to life. "In dead earnest," says Grimes, "Baum set about creating an amusement park for the senses." Managers were dispatched to Rome, Naples, Herculaneum, and Pompeii. The first century writings of Apicius, a Roman epicure, were studied. Classics professors lectured the staff on Roman history and culture. The menu was indulgent and pompous ("Filet Mignon, Caesar Augustus, with a Rising Crown of Pâté and Triumphal Laurel Leaf"), the décor decadent, and the wait staff clad in purple and red velveteen jackets meant to evoke the togas worn by Roman rulers. "The table is set with brass and copper plates," wrote *Life* magazine's associate editor in the April 7, 1961 issue. "The ashes from cigaret [sic] are deposited in porcelain trays inscribed with Caesar's head."

GOLDEN EGGS OF CRASSUS

As Mark, Veronika, and Peggy's family wait in vain for Peggy, Jerry studies the menu and remarks on "the oysters of Hercules, which you with sword will carve," reading verbatim from the real menu. We've selected another Roman extravagance from the Forum of the Twelve Caesars to add to our appetizers: the Golden Eggs of Crassus. This egg, sherry, and lobster meat concoction was named after Marcus Licinus Crassus, one of the richest men to ever walk the plazas of ancient Rome.

Golden Eggs of Crassus

ADAPTED FROM AMERICAN GOURMET: CLASSIC RECIPES, DELUXE DELIGHTS,
FLAMBOYANT FAVORITES, AND SWANK "COMPANY" FOOD FROM THE '50S AND '60S
BY JANE AND MICHAEL STERN (HARPERCOLLINS, 1991)

NOTE: You will need only six soft-boiled eggs in the recipe; two spare eggs are also soft boiled in the event the eggs break during preparation.

> *9 eggs (8 for soft boiling, 1 for the coating)*
> *(see note above)*
> *3 tablespoons butter*
> *½ pound lobster meat, chopped very fine*
> *2 tablespoons sherry*
> *½ cup tomato purée*
> *1½ teaspoons paprika*
> *Salt and ground black pepper to taste*
> *Oil for frying*
> *¾ cup plain bread crumbs*
> *6 pieces white bread, crust removed*

1. Make soft-boiled eggs: Place 8 eggs in cold water in a saucepan and bring water to a boil. Boil the eggs for exactly 3½ minutes. Drain hot water. Run under cool water until eggs are cold.

2. Gently crack each egg all around and carefully peel away the shell. The yolk will be runny inside and the white fragile. Set the eggs aside while you make the lobster sauce.

3. Make the lobster sauce: Melt butter in a medium skillet. Sauté the lobster meat with sherry, tomato purée, paprika, and salt to taste for 2 minutes. Remove from heat.

4. Toast the bread. To cook the eggs, heat 1 inch of oil in a

deep skillet to 360°F. Add salt and pepper to bread crumbs.
In a small bowl, beat the remaining egg. Dip each boiled egg
in the seasoned crumbs, then in the beaten egg, and then
into the seasoned crumbs.

5. Using a slotted spoon, ease the eggs into the hot oil. Boil
for about 1 minute, turning once gently, until barely crisp
all around. Carefully remove eggs with a slotted spoon and
place on a plate lined with paper towels.

6. To serve, top each piece of toast with warm lobster sauce
and place a single golden egg on top.

YIELD: 6 SERVINGS

MARINATED OLIVES

Every table at the Forum of the Twelve Caesars included a silver bowl filled with a wide variety of olives to whet the diners' appetite while they perused the menu or waited for a late-arriving guest—or even a no-show like Peggy. "There might be tiny black olives from Nice, no larger than a peanut," wrote James Beard about the Forum of the Twelve Caesars in *Beard on Food: The Best Recipes and Kitchen Wisdom from the Dean of American Cooking* (Bloomsbury, 1974). He went on to describe "huge luscious green Spanish olives stuffed with pimiento and the little manzanilla olives stuffed with anchovy; the long, pointed kalamata olives from Spain and California, sometimes called queen olives; and the soft Greek or Italian black olives preserved in olive oil after they are dead ripe."

The Forum of the Twelve Caesars "is a very fancy, plush place and the prices are very, very, high," wrote Minnesota restaurateurs George Leonard Herter and Berthe E. Herter in their self-published *Bull Cook and Authentic Historical Recipes and Practices* (1961–1963). "[We] would not advise going there unless you have money to throw away on very elaborate atmosphere." As for the olives, "they serve their olives…in the ancient Spanish tradition which is a good trick to know." We share the recipe from the Herters' book here. Just don't bother saving any for Peggy; she isn't going to make it tonight either.

Marinated Olives

ADAPTED FROM BULL COOK AND AUTHENTIC HISTORICAL RECIPES AND PRACTICES
BY GEORGE LEONARD HERTER AND BERTHE E. HERTER (HERTER'S, 1961-1963)

**1 *7-ounce jar green olives, pitted, stuffed or
unstuffed***
1–2 *teaspoons olive oil*
Garlic powder or onion powder

1. Drain the salt brine from the olives. Place the olives into a
   small bowl and pour olive oil over olives.

2. Sprinkle the olives lightly with garlic powder (use onion
   powder if you do not like garlic). Allow olives to marinate
   about an hour before serving.

YIELD: ABOUT 60 OLIVES

BARBETTA'S ROASTED FRESH PEPPERS ALLA BAGNA CAUDA

SEASON 4, EPISODE 8
"The Summer Man"

After their first date at Jimmy's LaGrange, where Chicken Kiev is the specialty of the house (see Chicken Kiev, page 201), Don Draper and Bethany Van Nuys visit a Benihana Steak House. This restaurant features a new fad in Japanese dining called *teppanyaki* where diners sit around a large cooking surface and watch the chef prepare their food in dramatic style (season 4, episode 5; "The Chrysanthemum and the Sword"). Bethany complains that the setting isn't very intimate, and the next time we see Don and Bethany out at dinner they are in the far cozier Barbetta.

Barbetta is the oldest restaurant in New York still owned by its founding family, the oldest Italian restaurant in the city, and the oldest restaurant in the Theater District. It is also the only restaurant in America to have been awarded landmark status by the prestigious Locali Storici d'Italia. Opened in 1906 by Sebastiano Maioglio, it is now owned by his daughter, Laura Maioglio.

If Bethany was looking for a more romantic and luxurious setting in which to charm Don than Benihana, this was it. Bethany is quite forward about wanting more from Don than the occasional dinner date, but he remains coy. They have one discomfiting moment at Barbetta when Betty and her second husband, Henry Francis, appear. But the evening is otherwise pleasant enough.

Each dish on Barbetta's modern menu is noted with the year the dish was first served there. Barbetta owner Laura Maioglio was kind enough to share her recipe for an appetizer first served in 1962: Roasted Fresh Peppers alla Bagna Cauda. We don't see what Don and Bethany have for a starter, but bagna cauda would have been a surefire way to warm up the evening.

Roasted Fresh Peppers alla Bagna Cauda is a variation on the full *bagna cauda,* a festive dish properly consumed with family and friends. Diners enjoy this dish by gathering around a table and dipping vegetables, principally cardoon, into the *bagna cauda* "sauce," which is simmering in a central chafing dish. *Bagna cauda* evenings are traditional in Piemonte during fall and winter, especially on holiday eves. (Italy's Piemonte region, the northwest region that borders France and Switzerland, is also known as the Piedmont.)

On the intimate cab ride home, it's clear that Barbetta is what Bethany had in mind for a romantic dinner date with Don.

Roasted Fresh Peppers alla Bagna Cauda

COURTESY OF BARBETTA RESTAURANT, NEW YORK, NEW YORK

For the Bagna Cauda

> *8–12 anchovy filets*
> *2–4 cloves of garlic*
> *¾ cup olive oil*

For the peppers

> *3 large red bell peppers*
> *3 large orange bell peppers*
> *3 large yellow bell peppers*
> *¼ cup olive oil (to brush over peppers)*

For serving

> *Red leaf lettuce, for garnish (optional)*

1. Soak anchovies in water to reduce salt. Strain, pat anchovies dry, and chop.

2. Cut garlic cloves into very thin slivers (adding more cloves will intensify the garlic taste of the Bagna Cauda). Pour olive oil into a heavy frying pan. Add anchovies and garlic and place over a very low heat. Cook, stirring, occasionally for 20–30 minutes. The Bagna Cauda is done when the anchovies have disintegrated. Set aside.

3. Preheat oven to broil. Cut each pepper in half lengthwise, remove the white ribs and all the seeds. Brush the peppers with olive oil and place in a baking pan, exterior skin side

up. Place under high heat broiler for 5–7 minutes. Remove peppers from baking pan and place in another pan and cover with plastic wrap. Allow to cool. When peppers are cool enough to handle, remove the skin.

4. To serve, place 3 pieces of pepper interior side up (one of each color) on a large dinner plate. Spoon 2 tablespoons of the Bagna Cauda into each half pepper (at Barbetta, lettuce leaves are inserted between each slice of pepper). Serve at room temperature.

YIELD: 6 LARGE APPETIZER SERVINGS

THE ELEGANT MAIN DINING ROOM AT BARBETTA ON WEST 46TH STREET

Salads

JACKIE KENNEDY'S AVOCADO AND CRABMEAT MIMOSA

SEASON 2, EPISODE 1

"For Those Who Think Young"

No one defined style and elegance in the early 1960s more than President John F. Kennedy and First Lady Jacqueline Bouvier Kennedy. As many have said, they were the closest America has ever had to royalty. Women looked to the young and beautiful First Lady for their fashion cues: from the hairstyles on top of their heads to the shoes they wore on their feet. Mrs. Kennedy's Prince Charming, the president, was young, handsome, witty, and debonair. Even those who were ardent Nixon supporters, and that included nearly everyone at Sterling Cooper, grew infatuated with the First Family and aspired to their suave and easy elegance.

Mad Men captures the public's infatuation with the Kennedys with great authenticity. On Valentine's Day 1962, Don and Betty Draper meet for a romantic evening at the Savoy-Plaza Hotel, looking every bit as glamorous as the First Couple.

After champagne, Betty asks Don, "Would you like another one here? What are we doing?"

"How does room service sound?" replies Don, who has taken a room for the evening.

Betty feigns surprise, but once in the room she tells Don, "I came prepared," and emerges from the bathroom in black lingerie, garters, and stockings. As sexy as she looks, however, Don has a rare moment of inadequacy.

"It's okay, we've got all night," Betty assures him and suggests they have something to eat. Don phones room service and orders vichyssoise and BLTs on white toast, but Betty takes the phone as the television comes on and we see Jackie Kennedy giving a television reporter a guided tour of the White House.

"Leave that," says Betty to Don, and asks room service to send something considerably more sophisticated, just as Jackie might have: half an avocado stuffed with crabmeat, a rare petit filet, and two place settings.

As the scene shifts we see that Salvatore Romano, Sterling Cooper's artistic director, and his wife Kitty are watching the same program, as are Joan Holloway and her future husband, Dr. Greg Harris (Greg is trying to make out with Joan, but her eyes are riveted on the television even as he lays her down on the couch). They were hardly alone; fifty-six million Americans watched Mrs. Kennedy's tour of the newly renovated White House as it aired on all three major television networks.

The public's sense of intimacy with the Kennedys is evoked the next day as Betty and her friend Francine Hanson chat while Betty folds laundry in her kitchen. Francine has been looking for a particular armoire, but has only been able to find "copies."

"Jackie has a real one you know," she says to Betty, then comments on the televised White House tour. "She seemed nervous. Even when she saw Jack at the end. It's like they were playing house."

From a distance at least, people were on a first-name basis with the president and First Lady.

In the summer of 1961, several months before her televised tour of the White House, Mrs. Kennedy had planned a state dinner in honor of Pakistan's president, Ayub Kahn, and his wife, and chose to hold it at Mt. Vernon, George Washington's home. Guests arrived in four flower-bedecked boats. Mint juleps (see Jane Sterling's Mint Julep, page 49) were served on the piazza followed by a dinner prepared by White House chef René Verdon. The menu featured Poulet Chasseur as the main course accompanied by a side of Couronne de Riz Clamart. The desserts were Framboises à La Crème Chantilly and Petits Fours Sec.

Before the main course came an appetizer Betty would have died for, and may have been thinking about when she ordered room service at the Savoy on Valentine's Day: Avocado and Crabmeat Mimosa. (In French cooking, the word *mimosa* indicates egg garnish.)

"The fruit known as the avocado is as adaptable as gelatin," wrote *New York Times* food critic Craig Claiborne in July 1963. "It complements crab meat and other sea food and has a natural affinity for tomato and onion, oil and vinegar."

This refreshing appetizer is adapted from *In the Kennedy Style: Magical Evenings in the Kennedy White House* by Letitia Baldrige, Mrs. Kennedy's White House social secretary, with menus and recipes by White House chef René Verdon (1998).

Avocado and Crabmeat Mimosa

ADAPTED FROM IN THE KENNEDY STYLE: MAGICAL EVENINGS
IN THE KENNEDY WHITE HOUSE BY LETITIA BALDRIGE; MENUS AND RECIPES
BY WHITE HOUSE CHEF RENÉ VERDON. (DOUBLEDAY, 1998)

2 ripe avocados

1 scallion, minced

2 teaspoons lemon juice, divided

¼ teaspoon salt, plus additional to taste

Dash of hot pepper sauce

3 tablespoons mayonnaise

2 tablespoons chili sauce

1 tablespoon prepared horseradish

½ teaspoon Worcestershire sauce

Ground white pepper

8 ounces cooked fresh crabmeat

2 cups watercress

2 hard-cooked egg yolks

1 tablespoon chopped fresh parsley

1. Peel half of one avocado. In a small bowl, mash avocado half. Add scallion, 1 teaspoon of lemon juice, ¼ teaspoon of salt, and hot pepper sauce. Stir until well combined. Reserve.

2. In separate bowl, stir together mayonnaise, chili sauce, horseradish, Worcestershire sauce, and remaining teaspoon lemon juice. Season to taste with salt and white pepper. Reserve.

3. Peel remaining 1½ avocados, cut into half-inch cubes, and place in a large bowl. Squeeze excess moisture from crabmeat. Add to cubed avocado and gently combine. Fold in mayonnaise mixture until crab and avocado are evenly coated.

4. Line bottoms of 6 chilled open champagne glasses or small glass serving dishes with watercress. Divide crab mixture evenly among glasses. Top each with a dollop of mashed avocado mixture.

5. Press egg yolks through fine mesh sieve; combine with parsley in a small bowl. Sprinkle yolk/parsley mixture evenly over each portion. Mimosas can be covered and refrigerated for up to 3 hours.

YIELD: 6 SERVINGS

See color insert.

THE GLAMOROUS FIRST COUPLE, PRESIDENT AND MRS. KENNEDY

SARDI'S HEARTS OF PALM SALAD

SEASON 2, EPISODE 5

"The New Girl"

When Don Draper and Bobbi Barrett meet for dinner at Sardi's, Don orders for them both: steak tartare (see Sardi's Steak Tartar, page 89) and a hearts of palm salad, another classic from *Curtain Up at Sardi's* (1967), which still makes appearances on Sardi's menu as a special from time to time.

Hearts of palm were once a high-end delicacy popular in the early 1900s at some of Florida's more luxurious hotel restaurants. During the Great Depression, however, widespread consumption threatened to wipe out the state's palmetto trees, also known as swamp cabbage, from which hearts of palm are harvested. Today, palmettos are grown as a cash crop and the hearts harvested when the trees reach a height of five feet. Only in Florida can you find fresh hearts of palm; elsewhere they are sold canned and packed in water.

Hearts of Palm Salad

FROM CURTAIN UP AT SARDI'S *BY VINCENT SARDI, JR. (RANDOM HOUSE, 1957)*

6 *lettuce leaves*
6 *whole pieces canned hearts of palm, drained*
    (about **21** *ounces)*
6 *thin slices pimiento*
6 *sprigs watercress*
4 *tablespoons Vinaigrette Dressing*
    (see recipe below)

Place lettuce flat on dish. Arrange hearts of palm in a row. Arrange pimiento slices across lettuce and decorate at side with watercress. Serve with Vinaigrette Dressing.

YIELD: 2 SERVINGS

VINAIGRETTE DRESSING

½ dill pickle, finely chopped
1 tablespoon finely chopped onion
1 teaspoon capers, finely chopped
1 tablespoon finely chopped parsley
1 tablespoon finely chopped pimiento
1 teaspoon finely chopped hard-boiled egg white
1 teaspoon salt
¼ cup olive oil
¼ cup white vinegar

Place the finely chopped ingredients in a small bowl. Sprinkle with salt and add olive oil. Stir thoroughly while adding vinegar. Keep in refrigerator. Always stir before using.

YIELD: ¾ CUP

See color insert.

OLD FASHIONED. SEE PAGE 11

MARTINI. SEE PAGE 13

IRISH COFFEE. SEE PAGE 19

MINT JULEP. SEE PAGE 50

CANADIAN CLUBHOUSE PUNCH. SEE PAGE 55

BLINI AND CAVIAR. SEE PAGE 78

OYSTERS ROCKEFELLER. SEE PAGE 84

GAZPACHO. SEE PAGE 95

CANAPÉS. SEE PAGE 104

AVOCADO AND CRABMEAT MIMOSA. SEE PAGE 132

HEARTS OF PALM SALAD. SEE PAGE 135

RIB EYE IN THE PAN WITH BUTTER. SEE PAGE 166

LUTÈCE GAMBAS AU BEURRE D'ESCARGOT. SEE PAGE 181

CHICKEN KIEV. SEE PAGE 203

PINEAPPLE UPSIDE-DOWN CAKE. SEE PAGE 219

PEARS BAKED IN RED WINE ALLA PIEMONTESE. SEE PAGE 235

THE PALM'S WEDGE SALAD

SEASON 3, EPISODE 2

"Love Among the Ruins"

Sterling Cooper copywriter Paul Kinsey is a Mad Man with a Bohemian heart. He grows a beard, smokes pot (and a pipe), and has liberal views. Controversially for the times, he also dates a young black woman, Sheila White, with whom he travels to Mississippi to be a freedom rider. During a meeting with executives from Madison Square Garden, a Sterling Cooper client, his political convictions lead him to overstep his bounds by a mile. To build a new Madison Square Garden, the owners want to demolish Pennsylvania Station, a precious New York architectural landmark, but community activists and protestors are opposing the scheme. "Rape of 34th Street," some call it. Paul offends the three Garden officials by siding with "the lunatics," as the executives call them, and challenging their plan himself.

To try and repair the damage, Roger Sterling and Don Draper later invite Madison Square Garden vice president Edgar Raffit to meet them at a restaurant for lunch. When Raffit arrives, he balks at joining them at the table, indicating that the Garden's relationship with Sterling Cooper is over. But as Roger, and then Don, work their magic, he sits down.

"Change is neither good or bad; it simply is," says Don to Raffit, and he begins to sketch out a plan to persuade New Yorkers that the new Madison Square Garden "is the beginning of a new city on the hill." When Don adds, "If you don't like what is being said, change the conversation," Raffit picks up a menu and we know Don has put Sterling Cooper back in the game.

When the waiter appears, Roger orders, "Iceberg wedges, blue cheese, bacon." The classic wedge salad was a ubiquitous entry on restaurant menus throughout the 1950s and 1960s, though variations of it date back as early as the 1910s. The wedge salad, which begins with a wedge-shaped slice of iceberg lettuce (so named for its ability to remain fresh when shipped long distance packed on ice), began to fall out of favor in the 1970s as consumers discovered other leaf lettuces—many more delicate and flavorful than the traditional iceberg—and lighter, healthier dressings than the fat-laden, cheese-based dressings that defined the wedge. Originally known as crisphead lettuce, iceberg has hung on, however, especially in steak restaurants.

Roger and Don salvage the Madison Square Garden account at an unidentified steak and chop house, so we turned to a cookbook from the Palm, a restaurant referenced in *Mad Men*, for our wedge salad recipe. (In season 4, episode 7; "The Suitcase," the younger staff of Sterling Cooper Draper Pryce go to the Palm for dinner and drinks before watching a screening of the rematch between Sonny Liston and Cassius Clay.) Served cold, a fresh wedge of iceberg (also known as heart of lettuce) may be plain, but it's always refreshing—maybe even refreshing enough to salvage a business relationship gone sour.

Wedge Salad

ADAPTED FROM THE PALM RESTAURANT COOKBOOK BY
BRIGIT LÉGÈRE BINNS (RUNNING PRESS, 2003)

NOTE: We added crumbled bacon to the Palm's classic wedge per Roger's preference. This recipe makes a large serving with two wedges per plate.

Make the dressing in advance. The cheese and the oil should stand together for approximately forty-five minutes, so the cheese softens and macerates in the oil.

> **2 iceberg lettuce hearts, quartered and cored**
> **1 large ripe beefsteak tomato, sliced**
> **Crumbled bacon, to taste**
> **¾–1 cup Blue Cheese Dressing**
>   **(see recipe below)**

1. Place 2 iceberg wedges on each of 4 chilled salad plates.

2. Top with crumbled bacon. Place slices of tomato alongside. Serve with the dressing on the side.

YIELD: 4 SERVINGS

BLUE CHEESE DRESSING

> **4 ounces Danish or French blue cheese, at**
>   **room temperature**
> **½ cup olive oil**
> **½ cup mayonnaise**
> **1½ tablespoons red wine vinegar**

1. Crumble the blue cheese into a bowl. Using a fork, whisk in the olive oil.

2. Let stand for about 40 minutes. Whisk in the mayonnaise and vinegar. Whisk again just before serving.

YIELD: 1½ CUPS

Carla, the Drapers' dignified, wise, and unflappable housekeeper, is a rock of stability in a household coming apart at the seams. She cleans, cooks, takes care of the children, and suffers Betty's occasional haughtiness while retaining a stolid self-respect. When Betty's irascible father, Gene Hofstadt, is forced to move in with the Drapers because of his early-stage dementia, he often confuses Carla with Viola, a maid who worked in the Hofstadt household. Carla politely but firmly corrects him.

The early 1960s, of course, was a time of great racial turmoil in the United States. The civil rights movement was taking root, but the world of Sterling Cooper floats serenely above it all with one notable exception. The only African American employee we see in the office building that houses Sterling Cooper, elevator operator Hollis, reluctantly becomes a focus group of one when Pete Campbell grills him about the type of television he owns and why he bought it. Pete is hoping to gain some insight from Hollis about sales figures he's reviewing for Admiral, an appliance maker and Sterling Cooper client. Admiral's television sales are flat except in predominantly black communities, where they are climbing. The executives at Admiral are reluctant to be seen as the choice of "Negroes" but Pete, ever practical, familiarizes himself with the market by reading *Ebony* and *Jet*, magazines for African Americans founded in 1945 and 1951, respectively, and urges Admiral to seize the business opportunity.

The civil rights struggle is evoked poignantly in several episodes. For example, in season 3, episode 9 ("Wee Small Hours"), we see Carla in the Drapers' kitchen listening to the radio as Martin Luther King eulogizes four young African American girls killed during the firebombing of a church in Birmingham in September of 1963. When Betty offers Carla the rest of the day off, she declines. "I hate to say this," says Betty, "but it's really made me wonder about civil rights. Maybe it's not supposed to happen right now." In the same episode, Suzanne Farrell, Sally's teacher and a woman soon to become romantically involved with Don, tells him she plans to have her students read Martin Luther King's "I Have a Dream" speech after we hear parts of it on Don's car radio. In season 4, episode 1 ("Public Relations"), Don dates a young woman named Bethany Van Nuys who tells him a friend of hers went to summer camp with Andrew Goodman, one of three young civil rights workers—James Cheney and Michael Schwerner were the others—murdered in Mississippi in 1964. And both Lane Pryce and Paul

Kinsey have interracial relationships, considered rather avant garde at the time. Even so, they are hardly colorblind: Lane refers to his girlfriend, a cocktail waitress at the Playboy Club, as his "chocolate bunny." The ever self-conscious Paul, always striving to hone his Bohemian image, even makes a trip to Mississippi with his girlfriend to engage in the civil rights struggle (season 2, episode 10; "The Inheritance"), though she breaks up with him when she becomes aware that part of her appeal is to burnish his liberal hipster credentials.

But it is Carla, strong, reserved, and dignified, who most embodies in *Mad Men* the separate world of black and white in the early 1960s.

One morning in September 1963, the confused Gene believes he's been assigned KP duty (he's a World War I veteran) and leaves a bowl filled with peeled potatoes on the Drapers' kitchen counter. That night, when Carla serves dinner to Gene and the Draper children, she has turned those potatoes into a sumptuous potato salad. For Carla's Potato Salad we turned to *The Ebony Cookbook: A Date with a Dish* by Freda DeKnight (1962), first published in 1948 as "A Date with a Dish," the name of a regular food column that appeared in *Ebony*. DeKnight, who developed recipes for food manufacturers and was *Ebony's* food editor, was one of the first women to advocate for African American culinary heritage. "There are no set rules for dishes created by most Negroes," wrote the author in a short preface. "They just seem to have a 'way' of taking a plain everyday dish and improvising a gourmet's delight." While her words may sound a bit dated to modern ears, when you taste Carla's Potato Salad you'll see that Freda DeKnight was spot on.

Potato Salad

FROM THE EBONY COOK BOOK: A DATE WITH A DISH *BY FREDA DEKNIGHT*
(JOHNSON PUBLISHING, 1962)

½ cup mayonnaise

2 tablespoons mustard

2 tablespoons sour cream

1 tablespoon lemon juice

1 tablespoon vinegar

1 teaspoon sugar

Salt

Ground black pepper

1 grated onion

½ cup chopped celery

½ cup minced parsley

2 hard-cooked eggs, cut into wedges,
*   or chopped*

2 cups diced cooked potatoes

1. Combine mayonnaise, mustard, sour cream, lemon juice, and vinegar in a large bowl. Add sugar, salt and pepper to taste, onion, celery, parsley, and eggs. Stir until well combined. Add potatoes and combine.

2. Cover and chill for 30 minutes before serving.

YIELD: 6 SERVINGS

KEENS' CAESAR SALAD

SEASON 3, EPISODE 4

"The Arrangements"

Pete Campbell's friend and Dartmouth classmate Horace Cook, whom Pete calls "Hoho," is a young man with an ascot around his neck and deep pockets filled with family money. His obsession is jai alai, a sport with Basque origins, and his ambition is to make the sport bigger than baseball. He describes his star player, known as "Patchy," as "Babe Ruth, only handsome."

At Pete's suggestion Horace enlists Sterling Cooper to create a media campaign to build enthusiasm for jai alai. Hoho's dreams are even bigger than his multi million-dollar fortune: He wants radio and print advertising and an adventure television series starring Patchy to air on all three major networks simultaneously and in color. Harry Crane, Sterling Cooper's one-man television department, notes that CBS doesn't do color yet, but that doesn't dissuade Horace. When Lane Pryce tells him the campaign will cost at least a million dollars, Hoho replies that's a third of his budget.

THE MAIN DINING ROOM AT KEENS STEAKHOUSE ON WEST 36TH STREET

"Enjoy your fatted calf," says Pete to Lane after the meeting. Pete has no qualms about taking his friend's money for a campaign he doesn't really believe will succeed; he's just happy to be making rain for the firm. Don Draper is less sanguine. He points out that Horace Sr. is "connected to Bert Cooper in a thousand ways," and won't look favorably on the firm exploiting his naïve son. Later, at dinner at Keens Chophouse (now called Keens Steakhouse) on West 36th Street, Don tries to steer Horace away from his jai alai dream (to Pete's dismay) because because he believes they are doomed to turn sour.

As they talk, a uniformed waiter prepares a Caesar salad tableside, the way

THE FRONT AWNING AT KEENS REFLECTS ITS HISTORY WITH THE PIPE CLUB, WHICH ORIGINATED AT KEENS IN EARLY 1900S

they still do it at Keens today. (Preparing a Caesar salad tableside was a mark of a restaurant's class; Betty, Don, and Roger enjoy one tossed tableside at Toots Shor's, another legendary New York eatery, in season 1, episode 2, "Ladies' Room," as well.

The spacious, high-ceilinged restaurant depicted in *Mad Men* doesn't resemble the real Keens, however. Founded in 1885 in what was then the Herald Square Theater District, Keens is far more intimate and clubby. Its low ceiling is lined with tens of thousands of clay churchwarden pipes, each numbered and carefully catalogued by a pipe warden so pipe boys would be sure to deliver the right smoking device to each one of the 90,000 members of the Pipe Club, a group that originated at Keens in the early 1900s. In the foyer at Keens are pipes used by such luminaries as Theodore Roosevelt, General Douglas MacArthur, Will Rogers, and, yes, even Babe Ruth.

Caesar salad has been on the menu at Keens since at least the 1960s, according to Executive Chef Bill Rodgers, and he graciously shared his recipe with us. Hoho believed jai alai would someday "eclipse baseball." He was wrong about that, but we're quite confident that Rodgers' recipe for Caesar salad will, like Babe Ruth, long be remembered as the greatest in the game.

Caesar Salad

COURTESY OF EXECUTIVE CHEF BILL RODGERS, KEENS' STEAKHOUSE,
NEW YORK, NEW YORK

NOTE: At Keens the waiters dress the salad and add the garnishes tableside. The recipe makes one large salad portion. You'll have leftover dressing and croutons. Executive Chef Bill Rodgers also recommends using this delicious salad dressing for marinating grilled chicken.

For the salad

> 3½ *cups clean, cut romaine lettuce*
> 2 *ounces Caesar Dressing (see recipe opposite)*

For the topping

> ¼ *cup finely grated Parmigiano-Reggiano*
> *cheese*

For the garnish

> *Pasteurized egg yolk*
> 4 *thin slices pimiento*
> 2 *anchovy filets, cut in half (4 pieces)*
> *Caesar Croutons (see recipe, page 148)*

1. Place lettuce in a serving bowl. Toss with dressing.

2. Sprinkle Parmigiano-Reggiano on top, garnish with pasteurized egg yolk, pimiento, anchovy filets, and croutons and toss well.

YIELD: 1 LARGE SALAD (SERVES 1–2)

CAESAR DRESSING

1½ *ounces water*

1 *ounce lemon juice*

¾ *cup canola oil*

¾ *cup pure olive oil*

1½ *ounces red wine vinegar*

1 *egg yolk*

6 *peeled garlic cloves*

10 *Italian anchovy filets*

2⅔ *tablespoons finely grated*
  Parmigiano-Reggiano cheese

½ *teaspoon salt*

½ *teaspoon ground black pepper*

1 *teaspoon light brown sugar*

¾ *tablespoon dry mustard*

¾ *tablespoon Worcestershire sauce*

1. Combine the water and lemon juice in a measuring cup and set aside.

2. Combine canola and olive oils in a measuring cup and set aside.

3. In the blender, combine the remaining ingredients and mix for 10 seconds. With the blender running, slowly begin to add the combined oils in a slow and steady stream. As you continue to add the oil, the mixture will begin to thicken. When the mixture thickens, thin it out with ⅓ of the water/lemon juice mixture. Repeat this process until all the oil has been incorporated.

4. Chill dressing until cold.

YIELD: 2½ CUPS DRESSING

CAESAR CROUTONS

NOTE: Place the bread in the freezer for 10–15 minutes before slicing to make it easier to cut even squares.

Whole melted butter can be substituted for the clarified butter, but will brown the croutons faster. To make clarified butter, melt 4 tablespoons of butter slowly in a small saucepan. Remove from heat and allow to cool a bit until it separates. Skim off the foam that rises to the top, and gently pour the butter off of the milk solids, which will have settled to the bottom.

> **6 slices white bread, crusts removed and cut
> into ¼-inch squares (see note above)**
> **2 tablespoons clarified butter, melted
> (see note above)**
> **1 teaspoon chopped fresh herbs (rosemary,
> parsley, and thyme)**
> **⅛ teaspoon kosher salt**

1. Preheat the oven to 350°F. Toss bread cubes in a bowl with the remaining ingredients.

2. Transfer to a baking sheet and bake for 10 minutes or just until slightly browned and crisp. Let cool at room temperature before serving. Store covered in an airtight container.

YIELD: CROUTONS FOR 6 LARGE CAESAR SALADS

KEENS' CEASAR SALAD

CONNIE'S WALDORF SALAD

SEASON 3, EPISODE 6

"Guy Walks Into an Advertising Agency"

At the elegant Long Island country club that hosted Jane and Roger Sterling's Kentucky Derby–themed garden party (season 3, episode 3; "My Old Kentucky Home"), Don Draper has a chance encounter with a man who identifies himself only as "Connie." Sometime later Don receives a phone call from a Mrs. Wakeman, secretary to one Conrad Hilton, the founder of Hilton Hotels and the owner of New York's famed Waldorf-Astoria Hotel. She tells Don Mr. Hilton wants to meet with him. When Don asks what it's regarding, she replies, "I just set his schedule." It isn't until they meet, less than an hour later in the Presidential Suite at the Waldorf, that Don realizes that the legendary hotelier is the "Connie" for whom he mixed an Old Fashioned at the country club.

"Food?" asks Connie gesturing to the table in the suite. "Best kitchen in the world. Got a salad named after it."

Waldorf Salad makes its first appearance in *Mad Men* when Betty Draper serves it as part of a luncheon for the parents of children attending daughter Sally's birthday party (season 1, episode 3; "Marriage of Figaro"). She could well have used the recipe from the *Hilton International Cookbook* (1960) as her guide.

THE MODERN WALDORF SALAD AS IT IS PREPARED TODAY AT ITS NAMESAKE HOTEL

In the foreword to that book, the real Conrad Hilton wrote, "As part of our program of acquainting people with the great food of all countries, this cookbook was put together to preserve in permanent form the most asked-for and most famous dishes of all the Hilton Hotels…A meal properly prepared and served can be considered an artistic creation, a masterpiece of which both the chef and the housewife can be proud." And a well-prepared Waldorf Salad was among those creations.

First prepared in the 1890s at the Waldorf Hotel, the predecessor to the Waldorf-Astoria, the salad's original recipe of chopped apples and celery tossed with mayonnaise is widely attributed to Oscar Tschirky (of Veal Oscar fame), the Waldorf's maître d'hôtel. His Waldorf Salad recipe appeared in his 1896 book, *The Cook Book by 'Oscar of the Waldorf,'* and did not contain nuts. He thought adding walnuts was an abomination. By the 1960s, the Waldorf Salad recipe had evolved and included nuts, typically walnuts or pecans, and grapes. Even at the Waldorf, the salad went through many iterations that included such diverse ingredients as smoked chicken, currants, Maine crabmeat, and crispy calamari. Other modern recipes now include raisins, watercress, and/or onions. Today, the Waldorf Salad served at Waldorf-Astoria includes chopped black truffle shavings and candied walnut halves.

Had Don accepted Connie's offer to enjoy the salad named for the famed Waldorf-Astoria kitchen, he would have been served the first version below, right out of the *Hilton International Cookbook*. The second recipe is for the salad as it is served at the Waldorf today. "It may not surprise you to hear that this is the single most frequently requested recipe at the Waldorf-Astoria from people around the world," wrote John Doherty, executive chef at the Waldorf, in *The Waldorf Astoria Cookbook* by John Doherty and John Harrisson (1996). "[T]his is my favorite version—it is light, refreshing, and the truffles give it that special touch. In fact, it is more popular now than it has ever been."

Waldorf Salad

ADAPTED FROM HILTON INTERNATIONAL COOKBOOK *BY THE HILTON CHEFS*
(PRENTICE HALL, 1960)

NOTE: You can use spices of your choice for the seasoned mayonnaise. We prefer salt and pepper to taste.

For the apples, we prefer a tart variety such as Granny Smith. Feel free to add your own favorite additions, such as grapes and nuts.

2 apples (see note)
1 cup diced tender heart of celery
5 tablespoons well-seasoned mayonnaise (see note)
Lettuce, for serving

1. Peel the apples and remove the cores. Divide each in half and then cut into slices. Reserve 6 slices and cut the remainder into thin julienne strips.

2. Combine the julienne strips of apple with celery and toss with half the mayonnaise. Place the mixture in the middle of a salad bowl and spread with the remainder of the mayonnaise. Garnish the rim of the salad with lettuce leaves and decorate with celery leaves and apple slices.

YIELD: 2 SERVINGS

Waldorf Salad with Truffles and Candied Walnuts

FROM THE WALDORF ASTORIA COOKBOOK
BY JOHN DOHERTY AND JOHN HARRISSON (BULLFINCH, 1996)

NOTE: You may substitute peeled celery for the celeriac.

The candied walnuts can be made ahead and stored in an airtight container. You can also use prepared candied walnuts.

For the candied walnuts

2 quarts vegetable oil

2 cups apple juice

½ cup honey

¼ cup dark molasses

¼ cup maple syrup

2 cups walnut halves

For the dressing

½ cup crème fraîche

½ cup plain yogurt

3 teaspoons freshly squeezed lemon juice

¼ cup walnut oil

Salt and freshly ground white pepper to taste

1½ tablespoons minced black winter truffles

For the salad

2 large Granny Smith apples, unpeeled

2 large Gala apples (or Braeburn, Empire, or other crisp red apples), unpeeled

½ cup peeled and julienned celeriac

½ cup celery leaves (from 1 bunch celery)

1. Prepare the walnuts: Pour the oil into a large saucepan and set over medium-low heat until a thermometer reads 375°F. Meanwhile, in a small saucepan set over medium heat, warm the apple juice, honey, molasses, and maple syrup. Bring to a strong simmer, add the walnuts, and reduce heat to medium low. Continue to simmer for 15 minutes.

2. Remove the pan from the heat and strain the nuts, discarding the liquid. Carefully add the nuts to the hot oil in batches and fry for about 20 seconds, or until they are mahogany in color; be careful not to overfry the nuts, as they will burn quickly. Remove the nuts from the oil with a slotted spoon and spread out on a cookie sheet lined with parchment paper to cool. When room temperature, chop the walnuts. Store in an airtight container in the refrigerator.

3. Prepare the dressing: Combine the crème fraîche, yogurt, and lemon juice in a mixing bowl. Whisk in the walnut oil and season with salt and pepper. Fold in half of the truffles.

4. Prepare the salad: Using a mandoline on the fine comb setting, julienne the Granny Smith and Gala apples into matchstick-size strips, being careful to avoid the seeds in the core. Transfer to a mixing bowl. Add the julienned celeriac to the apples. Gently fold the dressing into the apple mixture until well combined. Divide the salad between chilled serving plates and garnish the top of each salad with some celery leaves and the remaining truffles. Scatter the candied walnuts around each plate.

YIELD: 8 SERVINGS

Main

Courses

SOLE AMANDINE WALDORF-STYLE WITH JULIA CHILD'S POTATOES AU GRATIN

SEASON 1, EPISODE 2

"Ladies' Room"

Early in *Mad Men's* first season, Betty Draper gazes at her sleeping husband, Don, and asks the $64,000 question that will hang over every episode to come: "Who's in there?" Don is like an onion, and peeling back each layer only reveals another. Don has his own $64,000 question and asks it at least twice in this episode: "What do women want?" Well, fidelity, for one, but when it comes to Don that never seems to be on the menu.

When Don takes Betty out for a fine dinner in the city in the same episode, what she wants is tomato juice, a vodka gimlet, filet of sole, and potatoes au gratin. The restaurant isn't identified, but since its interior is suggestive of the Waldorf-Astoria Hotel's Bull and Bear Steakhouse, we turned to *The Waldorf Astoria Cookbook* by Ted James and Rosalind Cole (1969) for a recipe for Sole Amandine Betty would surely enjoy.

There was only one place to turn for Betty's potatoes au gratin: America's most famous "French" chef, Julia Child. No one had greater influence on the way American's ate in the second half of the twentieth century, and no cookbook was more indispensible than Child's *Mastering the Art of French Cooking* (1961), written with Simone Beck and Louisette Bertholle. The book not only created an appetite for French cuisine, but also incited interest in international foods in general. Child didn't promise French cooking would be easy. Rather, she wanted people to *appreciate* that fine food required some effort, a message that ran counter to the American postwar penchant for the conveniences of canned and packaged foods.

Betty probably would not have heard of Julia Child in 1960 when she and Don ventured into the city for dinner (Child burst onto the scene in 1961), but Julia Child's version of potatoes au gratin would have been a perfect complement to her Sole Amandine.

Sole Amandine Waldorf-Style

ADAPTED FROM THE WALDORF ASTORIA
COOKBOOK *BY TED JAMES (BOBBS-MERRILL CO, 1969)*

6 sole filets (about 6 ounces each)
All-purpose flour
½ cup (1 stick) butter
Salt
Ground black pepper
Juice from one lemon
2 tablespoons chopped parsley
¼ cup slivered almonds
Thin lemon slices, for serving

1. Wash filets, wipe dry, and dredge with flour. Heat one-half of the butter in a large, heavy skillet. Add the filets and sauté in foaming butter over medium heat until golden brown on both sides, turning fish once (this will just take a few minutes per side). Remove to a warm serving platter. Sprinkle with salt and pepper.

2. Add the remaining butter to the skillet and let it cook over medium heat until lightly browned. Stir in the lemon juice, parsley, and almonds. Blend and pour over the filets. Garnish with thin lemon slices and serve.

YIELD: 4–6 SERVINGS

Potatoes au Gratin

ADAPTED FROM GRATIN DE POMMES DE TERRE AUX ANCHOIS (GRATIN OF POTATOES, ONIONS AND ANCHOVIES), MASTER-ING THE ART OF FRENCH COOKING BY JULIA CHILD (KNOPF, 1961)

NOTE: This dish also works well cooked in individual serving crocks.

2 tablespoons butter, plus 1 tablespoon for top
1 cup minced onions
½ pound raw potatoes (about 2–3 large
   potatoes), peeled and diced into ½-inch cubes
3 eggs
1½ cups whipping cream, half-and-half, cream
   or milk
1 teaspoon salt
½ teaspoon ground black pepper
½ cup grated Swiss cheese

1. Place butter in a skillet and melt over low heat. Cook onions slowly in butter for 5 minutes or so, until tender but not browned.

2. Preheat oven to 375°F. Drop potatoes in boiling salted water and cook for 6–8 minutes, or until barely cooked. Drain thoroughly.

3. Butter a 3–4 cup baking dish. Spread half of the potatoes in the bottom and then the cooked onion and, finally, the remaining potatoes.

4. Beat eggs with whipping cream, and add salt and pepper. Stir. Pour eggs and cream over the potatoes and shake the dish to send the liquid to the bottom.

5. Sprinkle on the cheese. Dot with extra butter. Bake for 30–40 minutes in upper third of oven until top is nicely browned.

YIELD: 4 SERVINGS

AMERICA'S FRENCH CHEF

It's no surprise we see *Mad Men* characters frequenting French restaurants such as Lutèce and La Grenouille and eating French foods such as vichyssoise and coquilles. It was during this same period that Julia Child was, to borrow a phrase from the '60s, turning America on to French cuisine, starting in 1961 with publication of *Mastering the Art of French Cooking* (Alfred A. Knopf).

Public interest in French food was fueled in part by the Kennedys' passion for all things French. Distinguished French chef René Verdon was hired to be the White House chef, and Mrs. Kennedy spoke French fluently. But it was Julia Child, America's first true celebrity chef, who introduced Americans to French cooking, and there's never been another quite like her. The gangly, irrepressible cookbook author and TV personality became an American icon beloved for her wit, her authenticity, and, of course, her passion for French cooking.

Mastering the Art of French Cooking wasn't the first French cookbook to appear in American bookstores in the postwar years by any means;

there were many. Written by French chefs and professional food writers, the recipes were inaccessible to the average American cook because they assumed a certain amount of knowledge of French cooking. But Child learned her craft from scratch while living in Paris with her diplomat husband. *Mastering the Art of French Cooking* conveyed her love of the cuisine and the joy of learning from the beginning. It was a cookbook for the complete novice that broke French cooking down step by step.

Alfred Knopf, Child's publisher, had doubts about the commercial viability of the book from the beginning, and published it only after much in-house debate. Its authors were unknown and Knopf had just published a volume by Joseph Donon, a renowned French chef. Few resources were allocated for promotion. But when *New York Times* food critic Craig Claiborne gave the book a glowing review, the stage was set for Child to take the country by storm. She was invited to do a cooking demonstration on NBC's *Today Show* in front of four million viewers (she cooked an omelet on a hot plate). More favorable book reviews followed, including an endorsement from James Beard, perhaps America's most famous chef at the time.

"This is a book," wrote Child and her co-authors, "for the servant-less American cook who can be unconcerned on occasion with budgets, waistlines, time schedules, children's meals, the parent-chauffeur-den-mother syndrome, or anything else which might interfere with the enjoyment of producing something wonderful to eat." It wasn't just the destination that was to be enjoyed, but the journey. She was converting cooks into gourmands, walking her readers through the making of *boeuf bourguignon* and *tarte tatin*, and teaching that technique was every bit as important as quality ingredients.

Child took to the airwaves in 1962 on a program called *The French Chef*, produced at WGBH, Boston's public broadcasting station. *The French Chef* soon had a national following. With infectious joie de vivre, the imposing 6'2" Child wielded her kitchen knife with an equally sharp wit. On television, Child proved to be an outstanding teacher that viewers connected with. She wasn't particularly telegenic or polished, and her voice was given to warbles and sudden changes in register. But her movements were both flamboyant and buoyant, and she handled miscues, both in her presentation and her cooking, with humor and aplomb. In short, she was as irrepressible as she was irresistible. She was so comfortable in her own skin that she made others comfortable trying to do what she had done: master the art of French cooking.

TRUDY'S RIB EYE IN THE PAN

SEASON 1, EPISODE 3

"Marriage of Figaro"

One day the recently wed Pete Campbell gets a call at the office from Trudy, his eager-to-please new bride, who asks what he'd like for dinner. "Rib eye, in the pan, with butter," he replies. "Ice cream." When he hangs up he turns to Harry Crane as if he's had a revelation about the benefits of married life: "There's going to be dinner waiting for me when I get home," he says, sounding deeply satisfied. It's as if someone has just shown him the latest marvel from a clever inventor.

Pete is an ambitious go-getter with more than his fair share of chutzpah; he yearns to make his mark in the dog-eat-dog world of Madison Avenue. Pete's job at Sterling Cooper (and later Sterling Cooper Draper Pryce) is to make rain—to bring in the accounts that Don and his creative team will service.

"In a large Madison Avenue advertising agency," wrote Alan Koehler in *The Madison Avenue Cookbook* (1962), "it is impossible for one man to know very much about all, or conceivably about any, of these accounts. And even a top notch agency man gets just two or three good ideas a year, not enough to go around." Pete's rib eye in the pan sounded like one of his good ideas to us.

Still, his request that Trudy prepare the simple steak is a bit surprising. He apparently isn't familiar with *Life* magazine's *Picture Cook Book* (Time Incorporated, 1958). According to the good people at *Life*, Trudy shouldn't be anywhere near a steak until it's time to eat it: "Whenever a menu calls for a delicate dish or a fancy pie, most men are more than happy to let their wives take care of the cooking. When it's a matter of steak, this tolerant attitude is replaced by an unassailable belief in masculine know-how. Steak is a man's job."

Heloise Bowles—the über-popular newspaper columnist who shared countless household tricks with American homemakers (see Pat Nixon's Date Nut Bread, page 210)—suggested a "grand way to tenderize your meat. Get out your husband's hammer. Wash it with hot water and a piece of steel wool and *pound* that meat."

Regardless of who cooked it, there's no debating the popularity of the simple steak in the early 1960s; it was a red meat and potatoes time. "Not only do we serve more beef in the United States than in any other country except perhaps Argentine, but the pieces we use are larger," declared the *Ladies' Home Journal Cookbook* (Doubleday, 1963). "Sirloins and Porterhouses of our type simply do not exist elsewhere. In France, filet mignon is tiny compared with ours. In China, and all of the Orient the meat is cut into bite-sized pieces." Steakhouses dominated the New York restaurant scene and beef ruled the kitchens of women like Trudy, who were eager to please their hard-working, ambitious husbands.

Americans preferred their steak "super-sized" and cooked them differently than their international counterparts. "Two things that an American (as opposed to a French) cook usually won't do are: pan fry, rather than broil, a steak, and cover it with enough pepper to make Steak 'Schpeppervescence,'" wrote Alan Koehler in *The Madison Avenue Cookbook*. So Pete and Trudy are showing some continental flair, perhaps inspired by Julia Child who was at the time just introducing Americans of the era to the wonders of the French kitchen (see page 162). This recipe for Trudy's Rib Eye in the Pan is adapted from Koehler's book. The original calls for a sirloin or a porterhouse, but a rib eye will also do the trick.

Rib Eye in the Pan with Butter

ADAPTED FROM STEAK SCHPEPPERVESCENCE, THE MADISON AVENUE COOKBOOK BY ALAN KOEHLER
(HOLT, RINEHART AND WINSTON, 1962)

Steak (rib eye, porterhouse, or sirloin at least
1¼ inches thick, approximately ¾ pound)
at room temperature
Canola oil
Freshly ground black pepper
1 ounce cognac
2 tablespoons butter

1. Preheat oven to 500°F. Place cast-iron skillet in oven. Coat steak lightly with oil.

2. Spread ground pepper on a plate. Press the steak onto the pepper, and then lift it up and press the same side down again several times, until the steak is covered with all the pepper it will hold. Turn steak and press pepper firmly into meat with the heel of your hand. Apply pepper the same way on the other side.

3. Heat burner on stove to high heat. Remove skillet from oven and transfer to stove. Place steak in middle of pan and cook for 30 seconds without moving. Turn and cook for another 30 seconds, and then place skillet in the oven for 2 minutes. Flip steak and cook for another 2 minutes (3 minutes per side for medium).

4. Remove steak from pan. Cover with foil and allow to rest for 2 minutes.

5. While steak is resting, pour cognac into pan. Stir into the juices in pan. Add butter and stir. Pour sauce over steak and serve.

YIELD: 1–2 SERVINGS

See color insert.

A MAN'S WORLD

On a sunny weekend afternoon, Pete Campbell grills steak and corn on his apartment balcony for his wife Trudy, his brother Bud, and Bud's wife Judy (season 2, episode 6; "Maidenform"). We don't often see men cooking in *Mad Men*; that's women's work. But in the 1960s, grilling, especially meat, was considered a man's domain.

For those old enough to remember the early 1960s, it's hard to fathom that *Mad Men* is set half a century ago. A lot changes in fifty years and to a twenty-first-century audience, especially those who recall a world in which women cooked and cleaned and men went to the office and came home to be waited on, there are countless cringe-worthy moments in *Mad Men*. We suspect very few women watching the show think to themselves, "I wish I had lived back then."

Men and women had distinct roles when it came to preparing and consuming food in the early 1960s. Women may have sautéed the sole and steamed the asparagus but, grilling meat was a man's job. A woman had to consider her husband's temperament even when preparing food for the grill. In a 1964 *Life* article on preparing Chinese barbecued spareribs, the author recommended separating the ribs before grilling because the ribs need to be turned and basted on the grill. But, the author added, "If your husband does not have much patience, keep the racks of ribs intact and slice them apart after they are cooked." A 1965 *Life* article on preparing lamb chop shish kebab instructed, "An hour before dinner get your husband to light the barbeque fire—and make sure his fire is big enough to spread all the way across the grill." While women no doubt welcomed this "share the work" philosophy, lighting a fire was deemed men's work, too.

Grilling wasn't a man's only food-related job. Consider that a chapter in *The New Good Housekeeping Cookbook* (Harcourt, Brace & World, 1963) is titled, "When He Carves." A woman may have prepared and cooked the turkey, the roast, or the duck, but the man of the house did the carving. If goose, which is less meaty than turkey, was on the menu, a 1965 article in *Life* advised, "your husband should be warned that he may have to get all the meat there is off the bones." Not only was it assumed that men did the carving, but that only women read articles like this one.

By the same token, wives may have shopped, diced, sliced, and cooked in preparation for a cocktail party, but husbands typically mixed the drinks, unless they had daughters like Sally Draper around. A 1964 article in *Life* even suggested bartending was a matter of masculine dignity when it rendered this advice on throwing a dinner party: "And if you can manage it without hurting his pride this is surely the moment to move your husband out from behind the bar and install a professional." Ouch.

Because women in the 1960s were expected to shop for and prepare meals—when they weren't cleaning, ironing, sewing, or taking care of children—advertisers of food products took aim squarely at the fairer sex, as Sterling Cooper no doubt would have advised. A 1960 ad for Armour brand corned beef hash assured women it was "like the fresh-made hash that men order for lunch," and was "made the way men like it, with lots of meat." Pleasing her man was a woman's number one job, even when it came to purchasing canned goods.

As for cocktails? To a large extent they, too, were divided along gender lines. "Cocktails in the mid-twentieth century were gendered," according to *Alcohol in Popular Culture: An Encyclopedia* by Rachel Black (Greenwood, 2010). "Women's cocktails were frothy, colorful, exotic, and sweet, whereas men stuck to martinis, brown drinks, and straight spirits. The martini was a man's drink in its pure form, dry and bracing...Women's drinks might contain a plastic sword full of fruit slices, a tiny umbrella, or elaborate glass swizzle sticks." One need look no further for proof of this claim than the Mai Tai Rachel Menken sips as Don Draper enjoys a whiskey neat (season 1, episode 1; "Smoke Gets in Your Eyes").

BEEF WELLINGTON
SEASON 1, EPISODE 6
"Babylon"

When we first see Roger Sterling and Joan Holloway in a hotel room they've escaped to for one of their many trysts, Roger, who always travels first class, has a luncheon delivered to the room in an attempt to persuade her to stay the afternoon. Joan replies that she has to work, even if Roger doesn't.

"Aren't you even going to have any of this?" asks Roger. "Look, we've got Oysters Rockefeller. Beef Wellington. Napoleons. We leave this lunch alone it'll take over Europe."

"I don't like eating in here," replies Joan. "Food that close to the bed reminds me of a hospital."

We doubt anyone but a president or a prince was ever served Beef Wellington made in a hospital kitchen. It is a dish fit for royalty, one served at lavish state dinners, the finest restaurants, and the most elegant homes. If Napoleons are the emperors of desserts, Beef Wellington is the king of all beef dishes and Roger, who had already bestowed jewelry on "Joanie," was trying to make her feel like a queen.

Roger's quip about Europe may have had more historical substance than he realized, for it was Arthur Wellesley, the First Duke of Wellington, who defeated Napoleon at Waterloo. Though the history of Beef Wellington is murky, it definitely originated in Europe and it is generally agreed the dish was named for the Duke.

Beef tenderloin cooked in a rich pastry crust and "embellished with pâté de foie gras, truffles and cognac" is the gold standard for the dish as described in the December 26, 1965, edition of the *New York Times*.

"Beef Wellington was the premier party dish of the 1960s," wrote Sylvia Lovegren in *Fashionable Food: Seven Decades of Food Fads* (MacMillan, 1995). "It was rich, dramatic, expensive, and seemed difficult and time-consuming to prepare. In short, it was everything a gourmet dish should be." That it had European origins only added to the allure, especially as Americans began embracing foreign cuisines with more gusto.

Beef Wellington was also a favorite of President and Mrs. Kennedy, and was the main course served at a White House dinner on April 29, 1962, honoring Nobel Laureates.

Because getting the beef and the pastry shell right was such a challenge—

Marian Burros of the *New York Times* once wrote, after years of trying, that "a rare filet of beef and a flaky pastry are mutually exclusive"—some cooks outside the White House took shortcuts with the other ingredients. A recipe in *Vogue* in 1954, for example, suggested using canned pâté. And others, such as *Betty Crocker's Hostess Cookbook* (1967), from which our recipe was adapted, dispense with the foie gras altogether. But we did turn to *The White House Chef Cookbook* by the Kennedys' White House chef René Verdon (1968) for the pastry crust. If anyone knew how to get it right, he surely did.

We find it hard to believe Joanie could have said no to Beef Wellington, but imagine Roger found it almost as irresistible as Joan herself.

WHITE HOUSE CHEF RENÉ VERDON

Beef Wellington

ADAPTED FROM BETTY CROCKER'S HOSTESS COOKBOOK *(GOLDEN PRESS, 1967);*
PASTRY FROM THE WHITE HOUSE CHEF COOKBOOK *BY RÉNÉ VERDON (DOUBLEDAY, 1967)*

NOTE: You can substitute 1 pound of premade piecrust or puff pastry for the homemade pastry.

Beef Wellington typically includes pâté de foie gras, a paste made of duck or goose livers, and a delicacy in French cuisine. Although the pâté is not included in this recipe, you can spread ½ pound of pâté over the beef before covering with mushrooms and pastry if desired.

For the pastry

4 cups sifted flour
½ teaspoon salt
1 cup (2 sticks) butter
3 egg yolks
¾ cup cold water

For the beef

1 3-pound beef tenderloin
2 tablespoons butter, softened
2 tablespoons cognac
1 teaspoon salt
½ teaspoon ground black pepper
1 egg, mixed with 1 tablespoon water, for the egg wash

For the mushroom filling (duxelles)

1 pound fresh mushrooms, finely chopped
½ cup chopped onion
½ cup dry sherry
¼ cup butter
¼ cup snipped parsley

For the brown sauce

> *2 cups beef bouillon*
> *½ cup plus 3 tablespoons dry sherry, divided*
> *3 tablespoons finely chopped onion*
> *3 tablespoons finely chopped carrot*
> *1 tablespoon finely chopped celery*
> *2 sprigs parsley*
> *1 bay leaf crumbled*
> *⅛ teaspoon crushed thyme leaves*
> *2 tablespoons butter*

1. Make the pastry: Sift flour and salt on to a pastry board. Make a small crater in the center and add half of the butter, the egg yolks, and the water. Mix to make the dough. Chill dough for 1 hour.

2. Place dough on a floured board and roll into a square. Put the other half of the butter in the center. Fold all 4 sides of the dough over the butter to enclose it completely. Roll the dough into a rectangle 3 times as long as it is wide. Make a "turn": Fold the left-hand third over the middle and right-hand third over the left, making 3 layers. Repeat by making another turn and chill the dough for 20 minutes. Make 2 more turns and chill for 30 minutes before using. The dough will keep in the refrigerator for several days if wrapped in a dry cloth and a wet towel.

3. Make the tenderloin: Preheat oven to 425°F. Tie a heavy string at several points around the tenderloin. Place on a rack in shallow pan. Rub the filet all over with butter and cognac and season with salt and pepper. Bake for 20 minutes.

4. Remove filet to cooling rack. Let stand until cool, about 30 minutes. Remove string; pat tenderloin dry with a paper towel.

5. Make the mushroom filling: Combine all ingredients in a small skillet and cook until onion is tender and all liquid is absorbed.

6. Roll pastry onto aluminum foil into a 18 x 12-inch rectangle, ¼-inch thick. Place the filet top down in the middle. Spread mushroom filling over remaining surface of pastry, leaving a 1-inch margin on all sides. Draw the long sides up to overlap on the bottom of the filet. Brush with egg wash to seal and brush egg wash over top and sides of pastry.

7. Reduce oven temperature to 400°F. Carefully place pastry-wrapped tenderloin seam side down on baking sheet. Use the foil and 2 spatulas to transfer tenderloin. Remove foil. Bake for 30 minutes, until pastry is golden brown, or until the meat thermometer registers 130°F for medium-rare meat. Let the filet stand for 15 minutes. Serve tenderloin with brown sauce.

8. Make the brown sauce: In a medium saucepan combine bouillon, ½ cup sherry, onion, carrot, celery, parsley, bay leaf, and thyme leaves. Simmer for 30 minutes. Strain mixture through a fine sieve. Stir in 2 tablespoons of sherry, and simmer 5 minutes longer. Stir in butter, a little at a time.

YIELD: 6 SERVINGS

BETTY'S TURKEY TETRAZZINI

SEASON 1, EPISODE 9

"Shoot"

Jim Hobart, an executive at rival advertising firm McCann Erickson, tries to woo Don Draper into joining his organization by offering a higher salary, membership in an exclusive health club, and big-name clients. Having encountered Betty and Don at the opera, he also arranges to have Betty audition for a modeling job for Coca-Cola, one of McCann's clients. Though Betty believes she's selected from many candidates on her merits, it's part of Jim's effort to snatch Don away from Sterling Cooper.

After the photo shoot, Jim sends Don some of the pictures in an obvious attempt at a kind of blackmail. If Don wants Betty to keep the Coca-Cola job, he needs to make the leap to McCann. Don finds the tactic offensive, and tells Jim so during a phone call. "It's a pity to lose both of you," Jim tells Don and hangs up the phone.

At the dinner table one night, after Betty is told Coca-Cola is moving the account to London ("more Audrey Hepburn, less Grace Kelly," the art director tells her), she pours Don a glass of red wine and seeks to hide the news, and her disappointment, by telling Don she's not really sure she wants to work.

"I don't like you coming home to some whipped together mess of whatever's left in the fridge," she says, a reference to a casserole that sits on the table and a testament to what most married women of the 1960s saw as their principal obligation: being a good housewife and cook.

Don, unlike Betty, knows why she *really* lost the gig, but pretends not to know she's lost the job at all. He helps her save face and assures her that she has a job—as mother to their two children—and that she's the best in the world at it, or at least "in the top five hundred."

Mad Men creator Matthew Weiner identifies the casserole in the audio commentary that accompanies the first season *Mad Men* DVD set: it's Turkey Tetrazzini with fried Durkee onions on top. If you remember eating in the 1960s you almost surely remember having Turkey Tetrazzini.

We've adapted our recipe from *The I Hate to Cook Book* (1960) by author and humorist Peg Bracken. For women who, like Betty, were insecure about their culinary skills, or who secretly hated cooking, Bracken was a godsend. This mischievously funny cookbook, which was recently published in a fiftieth anniversary edition, could well have been the one Betty used to whip together her Turkey Tetrazzini.

"This book," wrote Bracken, "is for those of us who hate to [cook]...who want to fold our big dishwasher hands around a dry martini instead of a wet flounder, come the end of a long day." This was heresy in 1960, but Bracken was ahead of her time.

The I Hate to Cook Book came about when Bracken and some friends "decided to pool our ignorance, tell each other our shabby little secrets, and toss into the pot the recipes we swear by instead of at." She also wanted to write a cookbook that wouldn't make the average housewife feel inadequate. "Oh, you keep buying cookbooks," she wrote, "And, heaven knows, the choice is wide, from the *haute cuisine* cookbook that is so *haute* it requires a pressurized kitchen, through Aunt Em's Down-the-Farm Book of Cornmeal Cookery, all the way to the exotic little foreign recipe book, which is the last thing you want when you hate to cook."

Bracken dismissed fretting over what to do with leftovers. "When in doubt, throw it out," she wrote, but she understood it might not be so easy when the leftover was an expensive pound or two of meat. Her suggestion? Throw the leftover meat, whether beef, pork, or fowl, in with scalloped potatoes and lots of cheese, use it in toasted club sandwiches, or grind it up with pickles, onions, celery, and mayonnaise into a spread. As for leftover turkey, she offered a recipe for Turkey Tetrazzini. We added a sprinkle of fried onions on top to enhance this creamy indulgence.

Turkey Tetrazzini

ADAPTED FROM THE I HATE TO COOK BOOK BY PEG BRACKEN
(HARCOURT, BRACE AND COMPANY, 1960)

NOTE: Leftover roast turkey works well in this dish.

¾ pound spaghetti

5 tablespoons butter, divided

½ pound fresh mushrooms, sliced

⅓ cup all-purpose flour

2 cups chicken or turkey broth

1 cup light cream, half-and-half, or milk

2 tablespoons sherry

Salt

Ground black pepper

2 cups diced turkey (see note)

1 cup frozen peas, defrosted

½ cup grated Parmesan cheese

⅓ cup French-fried onions, for topping

1. Preheat oven to 400°F. Boil water in a large pot, and cook spaghetti according to package directions. Melt 1 tablespoon of butter in a medium skillet. Sauté mushrooms in the butter until lightly browned.

2. Make the cream sauce: Blend 4 tablespoons of butter with the flour in the top of a double broiler, then add the chicken or turkey broth. Cook, stirring until sauce is smooth and thick. Add the cream or milk, sherry, and salt and pepper to taste.

3. Divide sauce into two bowls. In one bowl, add turkey meat and stir. In the other, add the mushrooms, peas, and spaghetti and toss.

4. Put spaghetti-mushroom mixture in a greased, 9 x 9-inch casserole dish. Make a hole in the center. Pour turkey mixture
in the hole. Sprinkle top with Parmesan cheese. Top with
French-fried onions. Bake uncovered for 20 minutes.

YIELD: 6 SERVINGS

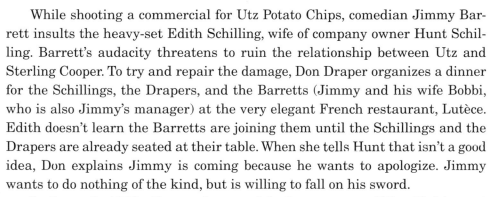

LUTÈCE GAMBAS AU BEURRE D'ESCARGOT
SEASON 2, EPISODE 3
"The Benefactor"

While shooting a commercial for Utz Potato Chips, comedian Jimmy Barrett insults the heavy-set Edith Schilling, wife of company owner Hunt Schilling. Barrett's audacity threatens to ruin the relationship between Utz and Sterling Cooper. To try and repair the damage, Don Draper organizes a dinner for the Schillings, the Drapers, and the Barretts (Jimmy and his wife Bobbi, who is also Jimmy's manager) at the very elegant French restaurant, Lutèce. Edith doesn't learn the Barretts are joining them until the Schillings and the Drapers are already seated at their table. When she tells Hunt that isn't a good idea, Don explains Jimmy is coming because he wants to apologize. Jimmy wants to do nothing of the kind, but is willing to fall on his sword.

In the early 1960s, the newly opened Lutèce was one of New York's most talked about, highly praised, and famous restaurants, described by some as "an outpost of Paris itself." Located on 50th Street between Second and Third Avenues, it was a stone's throw from the offices of Madison Avenue's most notable advertising firms.

The Barretts make a late entrance and Jimmy is his usual, chipper, one-liner-a-minute self. He interrupts the waiter before "Masseur Le Pew," as Jimmy calls him, can describe the chef's specials to order drinks because, as he explains, "Jimmy's down a quart."

"And make it fast," he adds, "while this place is still French."

When Bobbi excuses herself, Don quickly follows. "The window for this apology is closing," Don tells her. "It needs to happen before the appetizers or they will *leave*." When Bobbi tries to extort $25,000 for the apology, Don threatens to ruin Jimmy and Bobbi knows he can make good on the threat. They return to the table, and Bobbi announces that Jimmy has something to say.

"I'd rather eat your chips than anything in this dump," says Jimmy in the lead up to his weak apology. "They have snails here, you know."

While we viewers can't be certain what Don's party ordered for dinner that night, *The Lutèce Cookbook* by André Soltner (1995), Lutèce's first chef—who later became its owner—provides some ideas. In a nod to wise-guy Jimmy's quip about snails, we've chosen the *Gambas au Beurre d'Escargot* (freshwater prawns with snail butter). The name notwithstanding, no snails are used in preparing snail butter.

When Lutèce closed in 2004, Eric Asimov of the *New York Times* wrote what could have been its obituary. "Though it has been more than a decade since Lutèce was in its glory days," said Asimov, "the restaurant played a crucial role in the culinary development of the United States almost from the moment it opened its doors in 1961. André Soltner, who was the chef for 34 years and the owner for most of that time, was one of the first chefs in America to emphasize the freshest possible ingredients. While his nightly specials often included rustic dishes from his native Alsace, like a puffy onion tart, Mr. Soltner's cuisine evoked the classic elegance of the Old World."

Gambas au Beurre d'Escargot

FROM GAMBAS AU BEURRE D'ESCARGOT (FRESHWATER PRAWNS WITH SNAIL BUTTER), THE LUTÈCE COOKBOOK *BY ANDRÉ SOLTNER WITH SEYMOUR BRITCHKY (KNOPF, 1995)*

For the Beurre d'Escargot

1 cup (2 sticks) unsalted butter, at room temperature

1 ample tablespoon parsley, chopped fine

1 scant tablespoon garlic, chopped fine

1 tablespoon shallots, chopped fine

½ tablespoon Pernod (preferred), Ricard, or other anise-flavored liqueur

1 teaspoon salt

¼ teaspoon fresh ground black pepper

For the prawns

24 freshwater large or jumbo prawns, rinsed in cold water

1. Make the Beurre d'Escargot: In a bowl, mix together all ingredients until thoroughly blended. You may use a food processor, but do not overmix or it will lose its texture.

2. Preheat the oven to 450°F. With a sharp knife or shears, butterfly (split) the prawns and remove the vein, but leave prawns in the shells.

3. Place prawns shell down in a gratin dish. Cover them with the Beurre d'Escargot. Put the dish in the preheated oven for 8 minutes. Serve hot.

YIELD: 6 SERVINGS

See color insert.

SAL'S SPAGHETTI AND MEATBALLS WITH MARINARA

SEASON 2, EPISODE 7

"The Gold Violin"

The Vermont-born-and-bred Ken Cosgrove is a vice president for Accounts at Sterling Cooper—the business side of the agency—but he has creative and literary ambitions. He becomes the toast of the office when his short story, "Tapping a Maple on a Cold Vermont Morning," is published in *Atlantic Monthly*, and Ken learns during an elevator conversation that Salvatore Romano, Sterling Cooper's artistic director, really loved the story. "It was beautiful," says Sal, "and sad." When Ken, looking for critical feedback, asks Sal to read another story he's written, "The Gold Violin," he tells Sal, "I don't want you to pull any punches; unless you hate it. In which case, don't tell me. I'm kind of fragile."

Sal tells Ken he's honored and invites him to dinner that Sunday at the small but finely decorated apartment he shares with his wife Kitty. He'll have read the story by then, Sal promises.

When Ken arrives, a little late (after all, "he's a bachelor," Sal tells Kitty), he's holding a huge bouquet of flowers.

"Kitty," he says, "you could smell heaven in the street," referring to the rich marinara simmering on the stove. "I'd like to take credit," she replies, "but it's all the maestro." Sal asks Ken to sample his work, much as Ken has asked Sal to sample his: "Come, come," says Sal, "taste the sauce. Now tell me what you think. Be honest. I'm fragile." Sal holds up a wooden sauce spoon so Ken can taste his creation. "Better than a restaurant," he declares.

Most viewers will have already detected the debonair Sal's repressed homosexuality, and we are given plenty of evidence here that Sal's passions are simmering like his marinara. We can see it in the way he gazes coyly at Ken throughout dinner, the manner in which he lights Ken's cigarette, and in the way he pockets the cigarette lighter Ken leaves behind after heading back to the city. The dinner conversation, which has focused on Sterling Cooper, has left Kitty feeling ignored and sidelined, and she lets Sal know it. But it's Sal's subtle infatuation with Ken that's really gotten under Kitty's skin; she's only just beginning to come to the realization that her husband is attracted to men.

Sal's Spaghetti and Meatballs with Marinara Sauce comes from *Leone's Italian Cookbook* by Gene Leone (1967), the son of the famed Mama Leone of the eponymous New York City restaurant. (Former president Dwight D. Eisenhower penned the book's foreword.) Gene Leone credits Enrico Caruso as "the man most responsible for getting Mother to open her little Italian restaurant. 'Un piccolo posticino,' as he called it." Mama Leone's sat a mere twenty diners when it opened in 1906. Eventually, Mama Leone's would seat a breathtaking 1,500, and Gene grew "accustomed to cooking for from four thousand to six thousand people every day." Guests at Mama Leone's included Eleanor Roosevelt, Harry Truman, Marlene Dietrich, Rudy Vallee, Rocky Marciano, and one Dr. Aldrich. This last name belongs to Betty Draper's obstetrician, who was unavailable when she went into labor with her third child because he was celebrating his anniversary in the city at Mama Leone's (season 3, episode 5; "The Fog").

Spaghetti and Meatballs with Marinara

ADAPTED FROM LEONE'S ITALIAN COOKBOOK
BY GENE LEONE (HARPER & ROW 1967)

NOTE: You may use all ground beef, or combine 1 pound of beef, ½ pound of veal, and ½ ground pork. If using this combination, grind together so the mixture is well blended.

1 *slice bread*

Milk (about ⅛ cup), for soaking bread

2 *pounds ground beef (see note above)*

2 *eggs, beaten*

8 *fresh parsley sprigs, leaves only, chopped fine*

12 *chive leaves, chopped fine*

1 *tablespoon butter, softened and cut into small pieces*

6 *tablespoons freshly grated Parmesan cheese, divided*

1 *teaspoon salt*

Pinch of freshly ground pepper

¼ *cup olive oil*

1 *large onion, peeled and diced*

1 *small garlic clove, chopped finely*

2 *cups Marinara Sauce (see recipe opposite)*

1½–2 *pounds spaghetti, prepared according to package directions*

1. Soak the bread in a little milk, then squeeze out the mixture and shred the bread. Place the meat, eggs, bread,

parsley, chives, butter, half of the cheese, the salt, and the pepper in a large mixing bowl. Mix well with hands. Shape into meatballs 1½ inches in diameter.

2. Heat olive oil in a skillet. Add onions and garlic and cook until brown. Add meatballs and cook on medium-low heat until brown, turning so they brown evenly on all sides. Cover and simmer slowly for 45 minutes.

3. Remove meatballs with a slotted spoon, so liquid is drained, and place meatballs in Marinara Sauce and bring to a boil. Sprinkle remaining cheese on top and serve sauce over pasta. Serve extra sauce if you wish.

YIELD: 6 SERVINGS

MARINARA SAUCE

8 large garlic cloves, mashed
16 fresh parsley sprigs, leaves only
6 tablespoons olive oil
4 tablespoons butter
½ teaspoon salt, or more to taste
½ teaspoon freshly ground black pepper
6 cups (3 pounds) canned diced tomatoes
1 tablespoon dried oregano
6 anchovy filets
2 heaping tablespoons tomato paste

1. Chop garlic and parsley together. Combine olive oil and butter in a saucepan over medium-low heat and add garlic and parsley to the pan. Cook slowly for 5 minutes. Add salt and pepper.

2. Add the tomatoes with their juice and oregano to the sauce and cook slowly for 30 minutes. Add anchovies and tomato

paste, stir well, and remove from the heat. (If you prefer a smoother sauce, you might blend at this point by transferring sauce to blender or using an immersion blender). Sample at the end of cooking and add salt to taste, but remember the anchovies will make the sauce salty.

YIELD: 5 CUPS

TRUDY'S FLYING ROAST CHICKEN WITH STUFFING

When Pete and Trudy Campbell have trouble conceiving, Trudy makes an appointment for them at an adoption agency against Pete's wishes and has Pete's secretary Hildy put it on his calendar. It's from Hildy that Pete learns of the appointment. "I think it's one of the most blessed things," Hildy tells a surprised Pete, that "a person would give a home to an abandoned child." But Pete is having none of it.

He returns home that evening and Trudy has dinner on the table, including a whole roast chicken, but Pete is scorching mad. He tells Trudy they're not going to the appointment and they're *not* adopting a child: "Hell's bells, Trudy, that is final!" he declares.

Trudy yells that he can't speak to her that way, so Pete picks up the platter holding the chicken, opens the door to the balcony of their high-rise and sends it sailing to the street below. Hopefully, some hungry soul was lucky enough to catch it, bring it home, and declare it "take-out."

We found a delicious roast chicken and stuffing recipe in the "Special Occasion Dinners for Two" section of a small, spiral-bound cookbook that Trudy might well have kept on her kitchen shelf: *Betty Crocker's Dinner for Two Cookbook* (1958). After all, she was cooking for two most nights. Perhaps if Trudy had followed the book's advice and lit the two candles on the dining room table, she could have avoided all the unpleasantness. After all, candlelight, says Betty Crocker, casts "a happy glow over all."

Speaking of which, here's another piece of good advice: if you have news to share with your spouse that may not go over well, chicken is certainly a more economical choice than a fine cut of meat. Especially if there's a chance it's going to be tossed over the balcony rail.

Roast Chicken with Stuffing

FROM BETTY CROCKER'S
DINNER FOR TWO COOKBOOK *(SIMON AND SCHUSTER, 1958)*

NOTE: You may make stuffing ahead of time, but fill chicken cavity just before roasting. Make 1 cup of stuffing for each ready–to-cook pound of chicken.

Remember that the type of oven you use, your actual oven temperatures, and the tenderness of the chicken will affect roasting times. Check for doneness well before recommended cooking time.

> *1 chicken (approximately 4 pounds)*
> *Salt*
> *Butter, for coating*
> *Stuffing (see recipe opposite)*

1. Remove any pinfeathers and wash chicken. Rub cavity with salt.

2. Stuff body and neck cavities lightly. Stuffing should never be packed in. Place extra stuffing in a covered casserole dish. You can bake it in the oven for the last 30–40 minutes that the chicken is roasting.

3. Preheat oven to 325°F. Place skewers across opening and lace together with string. Tie leg ends to tail. Skewer neck skin to back. Fold wings across back with tips touching. Rub chicken with unsalted butter.

4. Place chicken on rack in shallow roasting pan, breast side down. When bird has browned as much as you wish, turn it right side up. Tent a piece of heavy-duty aluminum foil over the breast.

5. Roast for approximately 80 minutes to 2 hours (see note above), until juices run clear when a sharp knife is inserted

into the joint between the body and the thigh, or until an
instant-read thermometer registers 170°F at the same joint.

6. Remove the roast chicken from oven, cover loosely with foil.
Allow to rest for at least 10 minutes before carving.

YIELD: 1 STUFFED CHICKEN (APPROXIMATELY 4 SERVINGS)

STUFFING

⅓ *cup butter*
½ *cup finely minced onion*
4 *cups bread cubes, for stuffing (you may use*
  cornbread)
½ *cup chopped celery (stalks and leaves)*
2 *teaspoons salt*
¼ *teaspoon ground black pepper*
2 *teaspoon dried sage, thyme, or marjoram*
⅓ *cup chicken broth*
Poultry seasoning, to taste

1. Melt butter in a large, heavy skillet. Add onion and cook
until yellow, stirring occasionally. Stir in some of the bread
cubes. Heat, stirring to prevent excessive browning.

2. Turn into deep bowl. Mix remaining ingredients and rest of
bread cubes in lightly.

YIELD: 4 CUPS STUFFING

JOAN'S STUFFED CROWN ROAST OF PORK

SEASON 3, EPISODE 3

"My Old Kentucky Home"

For a dramatic dinner table presentation, it's hard to beat a crown roast of beef, lamb, or pork. Created from the rib section of the loin cut, the meat is tied in a circle and roasted ribs up so that it resembles a crown. The roast is typically filled with a stuffing.

Joan Harris née Holloway and her husband, Dr. Greg Harris, are trying to impress when they host a dinner party in their small apartment for two of Greg's hospital colleagues and their wives. One of the guests is Greg's boss, Chief of Surgery Dr. Ronald Ettinger, who will soon be deciding whether Greg will become chief surgical resident. There are martinis, and a platter of cheeses, meats, and crackers. Dessert will be éclairs, cookies, cakes, and coffee. But the main event is a crown roast Joan has made in her tiny kitchen.

Crown roast was party fare, or at least saved for special events like this one at Greg and Joan's. *The Small Kitchen Cookbook* by Nina Mortellito (1964), seemed an appropriate source for our crown roast recipe; Joan's kitchen fits Mortelitto's description of many found in modern New York apartments of the time: "The kitchens seem to be afterthoughts; they vary in size from a two-burner-oven-refrigerator combination carved out of the living-room wall, to a walk-in (but not sit-down) separate room."

The first step in making a successful crown roast is obtaining the proper ingredients, starting with the meat. Butchers needed, and still require, advance notice to prepare the cut. In *The Small Kitchen Cookbook,* Mortellito wrote about the importance of getting to know your butcher. "Some people believe that there are no longer butchers who will personally prepare an order. Not true. Somewhere, behind those coffers of pre-cut, cellophane wrapped meats, is a real live butcher who would be delighted to establish some human contact."

We suspect Joan's was a crown roast of pork; while speaking with the doctors' wives in her tiny kitchen she hints she and Greg live on a budget, and pork would have been the most economical choice. While we use pork in our recipe, you can substitute other cuts of meat.

Over dessert, Dr. Ettinger references a surgical procedure that Greg botched in the OR—a "bad result," as their other guest describes it. To cover his discomfort, Greg encourages Joan to play the accordion. Fortunately for Greg, Joan gets as good a result on the accordion as she did with her crown roast.

Stuffed Crown Roast of Pork

ADAPTED FROM THE SMALL KITCHEN COOKBOOK
BY NINA MORTELLITO (WALKER AND COMPANY, 1964)

NOTE: When you buy, keep in mind that most butchers will only sell a crown roast in multiples of seven as each retail rib portion contains seven chops.

   If you use a cut of meat other than pork, cooking times may vary.

For the pork

1 crown pork roast (2 lean, 8-rib sections tied together)

All-purpose flour

1 teaspoon salt

½ teaspoon pepper

1 teaspoon dried sage

For the stuffing

4 tablespoons butter

½ cup minced onion

¾ cup chopped celery

2½ cups white bread cubes

½ tablespoon poultry seasoning

½ cup chopped fresh cranberries

1 cup peeled, chopped apples

Salt

Ground black pepper

Parsley sprigs, for servings

For the gravy

2 tablespoons all-purpose flour

1 cup chicken broth

Hot water

Salt and pepper

½ teaspoon sage

1. Preheat oven to 325°F. Rub outside of pork roast with flour, salt, pepper, and sage. Place in a roasting pan, bone ends up. Cover rib ends tightly with foil and roast for 1½ hours.

2. Make the stuffing: Melt butter in a small skillet. Add onion and cook until golden brown. Place butter and onion in a large mixing bowl. Add celery, bread cubes, and poultry seasoning and mix thoroughly. Add cranberries, apples, and salt and pepper to taste. Toss until well mixed.

3. Remove roast from oven. Fill center of roast loosely with stuffing, and cover stuffing loosely with foil. (Place extra stuffing in a covered casserole dish. You can bake it in the oven for the last 30–40 minutes that the roast is cooking).

4. Roast for 2 more hours. Remove pieces of foil and roast for an additional 20 minutes, until the pork is tender, or until thermometer in thickest part of meat registers 185°F. Garnish with parsley. To carve, slice down between the ribs, serving 1 or 2 chops at a time.

5. Make the gravy: Drain off all fat from roasting pan and place in a small saucepan. Whisk in flour, and place pan over low heat. Add chicken broth slowly, stirring constantly. Add hot water, slowly stirring all the time until desired thickness is reached. Add salt and pepper to taste, and sage. Simmer for 3–5 minutes until gravy is smooth and heated through. Strain gravy if necessary.

YIELD: 8 SERVINGS

It's not often Don Draper is cooking, so we noticed when he makes corned beef hash one night in his kitchen in Ossining.

Shortly after Don and Betty's third child, Eugene, is born, Sally wanders into the kitchen to find Don frying some meat, diced potatoes, and onions in a cast-iron skillet. Betty is still in the hospital, so Don must fend for himself.

"What are you making?" she asks.

"A snack," replies Don.

"I didn't know you could cook," she says.

"Mommy's much better at it," Don admits, cracking an egg and adding it to the mixture.

Like Don, few professional men knew their way around a kitchen in the 1960s. They might cook a steak on the grill, but they weren't in the kitchen making soufflés or roast chicken. The simple corned beef hash Don is cooking up was likely the extent of his culinary skills. It is likely he even took the mixture straight from a can, as many did in the '60s.

"I believe that the ability to prepare and serve good food and attractive meals is a delightful *feminine* virtue," wrote Amy Vanderbilt in *Amy Vanderbilt's Complete Cookbook* (1961) (emphasis added). "The men in our family were all quite sure of their roles as men, which in my opinion is the way it should be. My father and my grandfather were never to be found in the kitchen mixing a cake." Nor, we suppose, making Miss Vanderbilt's corned beef hash recipe, on which ours is based.

Hash refers to the cooking of various odds and ends and comes from the French word *hacher*, which means to chop. According to *The Encyclopedia of North American Eating and Drinking Traditions, Customs and Rituals* by Kathlyn and Martin Gay (ABC-CLIO, 1996), "Corned beef hash...probably has its origins in being a palatable combination of leftovers. In the nineteenth century, restaurants serving inexpensive meals—precursors to today's diners—became known as 'hash houses.' By the early 1900s, corned beef hash was a common menu item in these places."

Though corned beef hash was more often served for breakfast, we understand why a new father, even one with two other children, might make a late-night snack of it: it's easy and delicious, especially when it's not right out of a can.

Corned Beef Hash

ADAPTED FROM AMY VANDERBILT'S COMPLETE COOKBOOK
BY AMY VANDERBILT (DOUBLEDAY, 1961)

3 tablespoons butter or bacon fat
2 cups coarsely ground or finely ground
corned beef
3 cups finely chopped boiled potatoes
1 medium onion, peeled and diced
¼ cup milk
Quick grind freshly ground black pepper
Eggs, for serving, if desired

1. Melt butter or fat in frying pan. Combine beef and potatoes in a mixing bowl. Add onion and milk. Mix lightly but evenly with a fork. Add pepper.

2. Place mixture in hot butter or fat in a frying pan and cook over medium-low heat. Shake pan occasionally, or lift meat on one side with a greased pancake turner. Press into skillet with spatula and continue to cook. When hash is well browned on bottom, after approximately 15 minutes, fold like an omelet and lift onto warmed platter. Serve immediately with poached or fried eggs, if desired.

YIELD: 6 SERVINGS

ROAST BEEF LOVERS... HERE'S YOUR HASH!

Mary Kitchen

makes it fresh from choice roast beef, oven-browned, then coarse-chopped into tender cubes—with savory pan juices and our private seasoning to give it an honest home-made flavor. Circle it with Hormel Bacon for baked Hash Filet Mignon. P.S. Mary Kitchen makes a superb *corned* beef hash, too!

Another fresh idea in meat from Hormel Geo. A. Hormel & Co., Austin, Minn.

A BUSY EXECUTIVE LIKE DON DRAPER, OR A BUSY HOUSEWIFE LIKE BETTY, DIDN'T ALWAYS HAVE TIME TO COOK UP CORNED BEEF HASH FROM SCRATCH. CANNED VERSIONS, SUCH AS HORMEL FOODS' MARY KITCHEN® ROAST AND CORNED BEEF HASH, LIGHTENED THE LOAD.

CANS OF HORMEL FOODS' MARY KITCHEN® ROAST AND CORNED BEEF HASH

BETTY'S SWEDISH MEATBALLS

SEASON 3, EPISODE 6

"Guy Walks into an Advertising Agency"

"Hot or cold? Swedish meatballs or chicken salad?" asks Betty Draper when Don comes home late from work on evening. Don chooses the chicken salad, but we chose the meatballs, thinking Betty's Nordic heritage might mean she knows a thing or two about preparing them properly.

Traditional Swedish meatballs are topped with a brown gravy, but over the years some in the United States began preparing them with a cream-based sauce. Often eaten as an appetizer, typically off the end of a toothpick, they can also serve as an entrée. When presented as a main course, they are often accompanied by lingonberry jam, cranberry sauce, egg noodles, or mashed potatoes.

Brought to America at the beginning of the twentieth century by Swedish immigrants who settled in the upper midwest, these bite-sized meatballs enjoyed great popularity in the 1950s and '60s, especially as an hors d'oeuvre, or as part of a buffet—*smorgasbord* in Swedish—or potluck supper.

Meatballs aren't exclusively Swedish; every Scandinavian country has its version made with veal, pork, or beef, or any combination of the three. The Scandinavian meatball tradition began as a way of using leftover meat—considered a luxury item not to be wasted—and there are countless recipes with variations in spices and cooking techniques. Some call for cooking in the oven, while others require pan frying.

A casserole dish filled with these tasty treats would have been very much at home at the Sterling Cooper Draper Pryce Christmas Party (season 4, episode 2, "Christmas Comes But Once Year") or at any festive 1960s occasion. There are countless recipes for Swedish meatballs from the 1960s to choose from, but we adapted ours from *The Boston Globe Cookbook for Brides* (1963).

Swedish Meatballs

ADAPTED FROM THE BOSTON GLOBE COOKBOOK FOR BRIDES,
EDITED BY NELL GILES AHERN (THE GLOBE NEWSPAPER COMPANY, 1963)

NOTE: You can serve these over egg noodles for dinner or alone as an appetizer.

> 1 *cup soft bread crumbs*
> ⅓ *cup milk*
> 1 *pound ground beef*
> ½ *cup finely grated onion*
> 1 *egg, beaten*
> ¾ *teaspoon salt*
> ⅛ *teaspoon ground black pepper*
> ¼–½ *teaspoon ground nutmeg*
> 2 *tablespoons butter*
> 2 *tablespoons all-purpose flour*
> 1 *beef bouillon cube, dissolved in 1 cup of*
>   *boiling water*
> ½ *cup light cream or half-and-half*

1. Soften bread crumbs in milk in a mixing bowl. Drain excess milk. Add beef, onions, egg, salt, pepper, and nutmeg and mix and combine with hands.

2. Shape into balls about 1 inch in diameter. Melt butter in a large skillet; add meatballs and brown over medium low heat. Remove with a slotted spoon to a baking dish.

3. Whisk flour into pan drippings and blend well. Cook, stirring constantly, until bubbly. Gradually add beef broth to the flour mixture, stirring constantly until smooth. Add cream or

half-and-half. Continue cooking for approximately 3 minutes, stirring constantly, until sauce thickens.

4. Add meatballs to sauce, and simmer for 10–15 minutes, stirring occasionally until sauce is of desired consistency. Serve warm.

YIELD: APPROXIMATELY 24 MEATBALLS

MISS FARRELL'S FETTUCCINE ALFREDO
SEASON 3, EPISODE 11
"The Gypsy and the Hobo"

After Don Draper becomes involved with Suzanne Farrell, Sally Draper's grade school teacher, their trysts take place in the converted garage apartment Suzanne rents not far from the Draper's home. Despite her initial resolve not to expect too much from Don, she begins to wish for a future for them as she falls harder and harder for him.

One night around Halloween 1963, Don is waiting for Suzanne in her apartment when she returns home with groceries to make him dinner. They embrace and Suzanne tells him she's making, "spaghetti, with cream and butter and cheese."

"And hot pepper," says Don.

"Yes!" exclaims Suzanne. "I had it like that in Little Italy. Oh, I love that place…I wish I could take you there."

Little Italy is New York's Italian mecca at the southern end of Manhattan. The area is crowded with authentic, intimate Italian restaurants, like Angelo's of Mulberry Street, a Little Italy institution since 1902. Though Suzanne was using spaghetti, and not the flat egg noodle about a quarter-inch wide known as fettuccine, the rest of the ingredients are pure Alfredo, a name derived from two restaurants in Rome called Alfredo that serve a pasta dish with the same ingredients. (South of Rome, fettuccine is called tagliatelle.)

There's no doubting the popularity of this Italian classic in Don Draper's time. A fettuccine Alfredo recipe published in the *New York Times* in 1962 was so popular with readers that famed *Times* food critic Craig Claiborne selected it as just one of three favorite recipes from 1962 to be republished in his column on April 2, 1963.

Angelo's of Mulberry Street has been using the same Alfredo recipe since the 1960s, and Chef Joseph Calle was generous enough to share it with us (it includes cracked pepper, as Don would have liked, on the side). The pasta at Angelo's is homemade, a step more ambitious cooks may wish to consider. A warning to the literally faint of heart: Chef Calle's preparation uses an entire cup of heavy cream *for a single serving*. As Roger Sterling says shortly after his heart attack, "All these years I thought it would be the ulcer. I did everything they told me. I drank the cream, ate the butter." Now that's rich!

Fettuccine Alfredo

COURTESY OF ANGELO'S OF MULBERRY STREET, NEW YORK, NEW YORK

NOTE: Angelo's uses homemade pasta and serves the fettuccine in a large bowl.

½ pound fettuccine
1 teaspoon butter
8 ounces heavy cream
1 egg yolk, lightly beaten
2 teaspoons Parmesan cheese, grated
Fresh cracked black pepper, to taste

1. Boil fettuccine in salted water according to package directions. Strain fettuccine and place in skillet. Add all other ingredients and sauté over low heat until thick, about 2 minutes.

2. Serve with fresh cracked pepper.

YIELD: 1 LARGE SERVING

In the fall of 1964, Roger Sterling tries to fix up the newly divorced Don Draper with twenty-five-year-old Bethany Van Nuys, a friend of Roger's young second wife, Jane ("Mt. Holyoke. Gymnastics Team...If you hit it off, come Turkey Day maybe you can stuff her," says Roger). Though Don tries to rebuff him, Roger tells Don's secretary to make a reservation for "Beauty and the Beast" at Jimmy's LaGrange. "They have Chicken Kiev," Roger says to Don. "The butter squirts everywhere." When they get to Jimmy's, Bethany orders the Chicken Kiev, and Don makes it two.

Jimmy's LaGrange is long gone, but it was a popular lunch spot for Madison Avenue ad men in the early 1960s. Its specialty was Chicken Kiev. Jimmy was Giulio Prigoni, an Italian-born musician who settled in New York. He often dispensed with menus and simply told customers—including Tony Bennett, Frank Sinatra, Gary Cooper, and Marilyn Monroe—what was for dinner. Jimmy would come to each table, draw Chicken Kiev (or the day's special) on the tablecloth with a pencil, and give a short lecture on how it was prepared and how it should be "attacked" with knife and fork.

Jimmy added yet another of the myriad legends surrounding this sumptuous dish by telling diners that Chicken Kiev was invented by Napoleon's chef during the march on Moscow. Winston Churchill once famously described Russia as "a riddle wrapped in a mystery inside an enigma," not unlike *matryoshka* dolls, the wooden nesting dolls that are a popular Russian souvenir. The same can be said for Chicken Kiev; its origins are also a riddle wrapped in a mystery. *The Russian Tea Room Cookbook* (1981) by Faith Stewart-Gordon and Nika Hazelton calls it the "most famous...of all Russian dishes," but acknowledges that its "Kievian origins are obscure and it seems most likely that Chicken Kiev was a creation of the great French chef Carême at the Court of Alexander I." Add to this the fact that Kiev isn't in Russia, but in neighboring Ukraine.

Other sources credit the Kiev style of poultry preparation to another French chef, Nicolas Appert (1749–1841), even though he didn't call it Kiev. These sources posit that the Russian connection lies in the popularity of French cuisine among Russian royalty of the eighteenth century who often hired French chefs or sent their cooks to France to train. Still others say Kiev-style chicken wasn't known in czarist times and is actually a Soviet-era innovation.

The style was often called "Supreme" in the United States, but it was New

York restaurants, seeking to appeal to a large influx of Russian immigrants in the late nineteenth and early twentieth centuries, that first dubbed the preparation "Kiev." After World War II, Chicken Kiev was a fixture in restaurants, such as the Russian Tea Room, that served fine Russian food.

The denizens of Madison Avenue would certainly have frequented this spot on West 57th Street, "slightly to the left of Carnegie Hall," where they might have been seated at a table next to Rudolf Nureyev or Woody Allen. The Russian Tea Room is famous for its Chicken Kiev, a fixture on the menu since at least the 1940s. This dish is adapted from *The Russian Tea Room Cookbook,* which says its version of this classic is "generally acclaimed to be *The Best.*" How do you know when Chicken Kiev is properly prepared? The authors of *The Russian Tea Room Cookbook* authors concur with Roger: it's "a spurt of butter at the first touch of knife and fork."

THE DINING ROOM AT THE RUSSIAN TEA ROOM ON WEST 57TH STREET

Chicken Kiev

ADAPTED FROM THE RUSSIAN TEA ROOM COOKBOOK *BY FAITH STEWART-GORDON*
AND NIKA HAZELTON (RICHARD MAREK PUBLISHERS, 1981)

NOTE: *The Russian Tea Room Cookbook* offers two methods for cooking the chicken. One calls for frying the chicken and the other for baking the chicken. We offer both methods below.

The cookbook suggests serving Chicken Kiev over a bed of hot cooked rice, with buttered vegetables.

> **12 *tablespoons sweet butter, chilled***
> **6 *chicken breast halves, tenderloins removed***
> **¾ *teaspoon salt***
> **¾ *teaspoon freshly ground black pepper***
> **3 *tablespoons all-purpose flour***
> **2 *eggs beaten***
> **⅔–1 *cup fine dry bread crumbs***
> **Oil, *for cooking chicken***

1. Cut butter into six equal pieces (2 tablespoons each). With your hands, shape each butter portion into a roll 3 inches long and ¾ inch thick (you can shape the butter inside a piece of waxed paper). Wrap butter portions in waxed paper and freeze while preparing chicken breasts.

2. Trim any fat from breasts. Lay each breast on waxed paper, cover with another sheet of waxed paper, and with a mallet or rolling pin pound meat to ⅛-inch thickness. Pound meat as thin as possible at the edges since the thinner the edges, the easier it will be to seal them firmly to prevent butter from oozing out during cooking. Be careful not to tear the meat. Each pounded breast should be approximately 8 inches long and 5 inches wide.

3. To assemble, gently peel off the waxed paper from each breast. Sprinkle one side of each breast with salt and pepper. Place one piece of butter in the center of the chicken breast. Fold two sides over the butter. Fold one end of the breast and roll up the rest of the way.

4. Coat each cutlet on all sides with flour, shaking off excess. Dip lightly into beaten eggs, shaking off excess. Roll in bread crumbs, coating the cutlets evenly and shaking off the excess. Place cutlets in one layer on a platter, cover with plastic wrap and refrigerate for 1–2 hours.

5. Heat oil in a large heavy saucepan or fryer; the oil should reach 3–4 inches up side of pan. Heat until oil registers 360°F on a thermometer or until a 1-inch bread cube dropped into the hot oil turns golden in slightly less than a minute. Fry 3 cutlets at a time in hot oil until golden brown. The cutlets should not touch each other during frying. Turn twice, using tongs or 2 spoons for turning and for removing the cutlets from the hot oil; this will prevent their being pierced. Drain on paper towels and transfer to heated serving dish.

Alternative method: Preheat oven to 350°F. Fry cutlets for 3 minutes, turning once. Place cutlets in a 13 x 9 x 2-inch baking pan and cook uncovered for about 15 minutes. Turn over twice while cooking using tongs or two spoons. Drain on paper towels before serving.

YIELD: 6 SERVINGS

See color insert.

"Ham is the homemaker's delight," declared an article in *Woman's Day* magazine in April 1961. "You can dress it up for a holiday meal or down for hearty, simple family fare."

Just before Thanksgiving 1964, Pete Campbell drops a Sugarberry canned ham on Peggy Olson's desk.

"Happy Thanksgiving," says Pete, sounding not at all happy.

"Oooh," Peggy replies, "my mother is going to be over the moon."

"Enjoy it," Pete counters. "It's the last thing we're going to get from them." Pete fears they're going to lose the Sugarberry account because of the creative department's lackluster work.

One dish Peggy's mother might have made with her Sugarberry ham is pineapple glazed ham, a popular dish in the 1960s that makes at least two appearances in *Mad Men*. In season 1, episode 9 ("Shoot"), Don spies a pineapple-glazed ham on the top rack of the fridge when Betty fixes him a late-night snack.

"Look at that!" he exclaims.

"It's raw," Betty informs him, so he has to settle for a sandwich.

There's also a pineapple-glazed ham on the dinner table when Joan Harris makes a Hawaiian-themed New Year's Eve dinner for husband Greg in season 4, episode 3 ("The Good News"). Joan's ham looks like it could feed a dozen, but there are just two of them at the table. Luckily for Joan, "the ham remaining after the first meal is no leftover in the usual sense," according to *Woman's Day*. "There are dozens of things to be done with it, each a new dish with nothing to indicate it had its origin in last Sunday's dinner." Whether reheated or cold, sliced or in chunks or strips, *Woman's Day* assured readers that the entire ham could be used later, "so there's not a penny's waste in your purchase."

Glazed hams have a long history in the United States going all the way back to George Washington. Washington had a smokehouse at Mt. Vernon, his Virginia residence, where Martha Washington closely supervised the preparation of meats served to their guests. One of the president's favorite dishes was a smoked ham with a sweet glaze. Honey glazes have long been popular, as evidenced by a recipe for honey-glazed baked ham in *Mrs. Beeton's Book of Household Management*, an English classic published in 1861. As for pairing pineapple with ham, that appears to be a part of America's love affair with the Hawaiian Islands that started shortly before Hawaii was admitted to the Union—as the fiftieth state—

in 1959. This interest continued well into the 1960s and pops up on episodes throughout each of *Mad Men's* seasons (see Joan's Blue Hawaii, page 60).

You won't find Sugarberry hams at your local grocery store—they never existed—but there are many other good brands to choose from.

Pineapple-Glazed Ham

ADAPTED FROM THE NEW GOOD HOUSEKEEPING COOKBOOK *(HEARST 1963)*

1 *ham*
1 *cup pineapple juice, or reserved juice from
    pineapple can*
¾ *cup brown sugar*
1 *teaspoon dry mustard*
1 *15-ounce can pineapple slices*
Maraschino cherries, optional

1. Cook ham according to instructions on the package. Remove ham from oven 45 minutes before it is done cooking and remove rind. Score ham, if you wish, by cutting it in long diagonal slashes in one direction and then crossing those cuts with diagonal slashes in the opposite direction to create a diamond pattern. Increase oven temperature to 400°F.

2. Combine pineapple juice, brown sugar, and mustard in a small saucepan. Cook over low heat until thickened and clear. Spread on ham. Use toothpicks to fasten pineapple slices to ham, and place maraschino cherries inside the pineapple rings. Return to oven for 20 minutes, or until pineapple is glazed.

3. Place fully cooked ham on a serving platter and let rest for 15 minutes before carving into thin slices.

YIELD: 1 HAM

ts and

s

PAT NIXON'S DATE NUT BREAD

SEASON 1, EPISODE 3

"Marriage of Figaro"

All the neighbors and their children are invited to Sally Draper's sixth birthday party at the Draper home in Ossining. For the children, the fare is that all-American classic, the peanut butter and jelly sandwich. Entertaining for adults was a more serious affair in the world of *Mad Men*, however, and always involved copious amounts of alcohol. As Betty enters the dining room crowded with guests she carries a tray of mint juleps (see Jane Sterling's Mint Julep, page 49). "It's that time of year," says Betty. Then she announces the menu for the adults: Waldorf salad (see Connie's Waldorf Salad, page 150), cold turkey, stuffed celery (see Betty's Stuffed Celery, page 72), and date nut bread.

It's the summer of 1960, just months before the presidential election, and Sterling Cooper is angling for the Nixon campaign's business. This is the first election in U.S. history in which advertising and television, are playing a major role in what author Joe McGinniss famously called "the selling of the president." Sterling Cooper is a Republican stronghold through and through; if there's a Kennedy supporter in the firm he (or she) is keeping it a secret.

In 1961, Pat Nixon, the former second lady and future first lady, shared her recipe for date nut bread with Heloise Bowles, the creator of one of the most successful syndicated columns in the history of American journalism. "Hints from Heloise" appeared in

FIRST LADY PAT NIXON

more than 600 newspapers in the 1960s and offered advice for housewives on everything from saving money to housekeeping. Betty Draper didn't have Pat

Nixon's recipe in 1960, but she almost certainly would have been reading Heloise Bowles' syndicated newspaper column, just as millions of American housewives did. Heloise validated them in no uncertain terms: "You, the homemaker, are the backbone of the world," she wrote in *Heloise's Kitchen Hints* (Prentice-Hall, 1963). "If it weren't for you there would be no home, no family, or world fit to live in." And no Pat Nixon's Date Nut Bread, either.

Date nut bread makes an encore appearance in season 3, episode 10 ("The Color Blue"). Suzanne Farrell, the schoolteacher with whom Don has an affair, bakes three loaves of it for a bake sale, but keeps one to share with Don. The next morning Don enjoys a piece of Miss Farrell's creation at the office as his creative team presents advertising ideas for a client called Aquanet. The bread is Don's reminder of the sweet night before.

Date Nut Bread

ADAPTED FROM PAT NIXON'S RECIPE IN
"HINTS FROM HELOISE" NEWSPAPER COLUMN, 1961

NOTE: You can substitute 2 tablespoons of brown sugar for 2 tablespoons of the granulated sugar.

8 ounces pitted dates, chopped into small pieces
1 teaspoon baking soda
¾ cup boiling water
4 tablespoons butter
¾ cup sugar (see note above)
1 egg
1¼ cups all-purpose flour
¾ cup chopped walnuts
½ teaspoon vanilla extract

1. Preheat oven to a 350°F. Grease and flour an 8 x 4 x 2½-inch loaf pan.

2. Place dates in a large bowl. Add baking soda to boiling water and pour over dates in bowl. Set aside and let mixture stand while mixing other ingredients.

3. In the bowl of an electric mixer, cream butter and sugar. Add the egg and mix well. Strain water from the date mixture into batter. Add flour and beat well. Add nuts, dates, and vanilla and combine until all ingredients are well mixed.

4. Pour the mixture into greased loaf pan. Bake for 50–60 minutes, or until toothpick inserted in center of bread comes out clean.

YIELD: 1 LOAF

SALLY'S COCOA FUDGE CAKE

SEASON 1, EPISODE 7

"Red in the Face"

One evening after work, while having a drink at the Oak Bar (see Oak Bar Manhattan, page 65), Roger Sterling hints strongly to Don Draper that he'd enjoy a home-cooked meal; his wife, Mona, has mostly stopped cooking. Don takes the hint and phones Betty to tell her Roger will be joining them. She is caught unprepared but, when it's 1960 and your husband tells you his boss is coming for dinner, you make do. As Roger and Don enjoy steak, green beans, and mashed potatoes, Betty nibbles at a salad. "You sure you won't have some?" asks Roger. Betty assures him she has to watch what she eats because she was once overweight as a child.

Dessert is a chocolate cake, made by the Draper's young daughter Sally, who, Betty tells Roger, just received a frosting machine. Written in frosting on the cake are the words "Mommy and Daddy."

After dinner, and no small amount of vodka, Don suggests "a commercial break, brought to you by more liquor." Many cigarettes are smoked and Roger begins to tell war stories, literally, of his time as a soldier in the Second World War. When Don heads out to the garage for another bottle of booze, Roger follows Betty into the kitchen.

"Sally will be happy her cake was such a hit," says Betty.

Roger, never at a loss for a double entendre, replies, "Make sure you tell her I ate the 'M' in 'Mommy,'" and with that makes a pass at Betty that she rebuffs.

This simple cake is adapted from *Betty Crocker's New Boys and Girls Cookbook* (1965). The first edition appeared in 1957, and Sally might well have used both her new frosting machine and her Betty Crocker cookbook to whip up this sweet concoction. (We think it was the liquor, and not the cake, that put Roger in an amorous mood. It may have been a combination of the two, though, so serve wisely.)

Cocoa Fudge Cake

ADAPTED FROM BETTY CROCKER'S NEW BOYS AND GIRLS COOKBOOK
(WESTERN PUBLISHING COMPANY, INC., 1965)

1⅔ cups all-purpose flour

1½ cups sugar

⅔ cups unsweetened cocoa powder

1½ teaspoons baking soda

1 teaspoon salt

½ cup butter, softened

1½ cups buttermilk

1 teaspoon vanilla extract

2 eggs

Quick Fudge Frosting (see recipe opposite)

1. Preheat oven to 350°F. Grease and flour a 13x9½x2-inch pan.

2. Stir flour, sugar, cocoa, baking soda, and salt together in mixing bowl.

3. Add butter, buttermilk, and vanilla. Beat for 2 minutes at medium speed using an electric mixer, or 300 strokes by hand. If you use an electric mixer, scrape the sides and bottom of bowl often with a rubber scraper.

4. Add eggs. Beat for 2 minutes more, scraping bottom and sides of bowl often.

5. Pour into prepared pan and bake for 25 minutes. Cool in pan on wire rack.

6. Frost with Quick Fudge Frosting.

QUICK FUDGE FROSTING

1 cup granulated sugar

¼ cup unsweetened cocoa powder

4 tablespoons (¼ cup) butter

½ cup milk

2 tablespoons light corn syrup

1½ cups sifted confectioners' sugar

1 teaspoon vanilla extract

1. Mix sugar and cocoa in medium saucepan. Add butter, milk, and corn syrup. Bring to a boil. Boil for 3 minutes, stirring occasionally. Remove from heat. Set pan in cold water.

2. When the syrup is cool, stir in confectioners' sugar and vanilla. If frosting is too thin, add a little more confectioners' sugar and vanilla. If frosting is too thick, add a little more milk.

BETTY'S COOKBOOKS

Two best-selling cookbooks of the 1960s appear regularly on Betty Draper's kitchen counter: the *Better Homes and Gardens New Cook Book*, first published in 1930 and revised and republished in 1962, and *Betty Crocker's Hostess Cookbook*, first published in 1967. *Betty Crocker's Hostess Cookbook* didn't exist when the first four seasons of *Mad Men* are set, but these two colorful books were in fact sensationally popular during the decade.

By 1962, the *Better Homes and Gardens New Cook Book* had sold more than 11 million copies. (It has today sold more than 40 million.) Its design was innovative. The pages were secured in a compact ringed binder so they could be removed and taken to the market. Sections were tabbed for easy use and it lay flat and stayed open, no small matter as anyone who has ever tried to prop a thick cookbook open on a counter can attest. The book's red plaid cover itself has become an icon, and the book, now in its fifteenth edition, is sometimes referred to as the "Red Plaids."

Betty Crocker's Hostess Cookbook was one of many in the Betty Crocker series of cookbooks that were enormously popular in the mid-twentieth century. More than a cookbook, in one slim volume it promised to tell a housewife everything she needed to know about "today's entertaining." It was filled with information on party planning, presentation, and managing special situations such as cooking for dieters and children. Also spiral bound, it featured more than 400 recipes and promised to boost the confidence of women who were insecure about their culinary skills.

Betty Crocker, who came to embody the concept of the American housewife, was not a real person. The Washburn Crosby Company, a predecessor company to General Mills (which currently owns the Betty Crocker trademark and brand) first used the name "Betty Crocker" in 1921 as a way of personalizing answers to questions posed by consumers. "Crocker" was borrowed from one of the company's directors, and the name "Betty" was selected because it was seen as uplifting and quintessentially American.

"So don't let inexperience, shyness or a tiny kitchen stop you," read a letter from the mythical Betty Crocker printed on the cookbook's inside cover. "Pick a party, and start planning now. One star performance will lead to another, each a little easier and perhaps a bit more elaborate than the last. May every one be a smash hit!"

KITTY'S PINEAPPLE UPSIDE-DOWN CAKE

SEASON 2, EPISODE 1

"For Those Who Think Young"

As Don and Betty Draper celebrate Valentine's Day 1962 at New York's Savoy-Plaza Hotel, ordering room service and watching Jackie Kennedy's televised White House tour (see Jackie Kennedy's Avocado and Crabmeat Mimosa, page 130), Salvatore Romano and his wife Kitty are watching the same program in their New York apartment. The dessert Sal and Kitty are enjoying in front of the TV is an American classic: pineapple upside-down cake, so-named because the fruit, sugar, and butter are put in the pan or skillet first, the batter poured over them, and the cake flipped over on a plate for serving.

Upside down cakes date to the late 1800s when cooks used skillets to make cakes because ovens were not yet reliable. But the pineapple upside-down cake first appeared in the 1920s when Jim Dole, founder of the Hawaiian Pineapple Company (later the Dole Food Co.), started canning up to 95 percent of his crop. This practice brought the once exotic fruit into the mainstream. When Dole Food Co. held a cooking with pineapple contest in 1926, more than 2,500 of the submissions were for pineapple upside-down cake.

Just as new foods inspired new recipes, new kitchen appliances inspired new ways to make them and cookbooks reflected the trend. "Cooking in an electric skillet or frypan (the words are synonymous here) is cooking at its best," wrote Roberta Ames in *The Complete Electric Skillet-Frypan Cookbook* (1960), one of many period cookbooks designed entirely around a new kitchen technology. "I can think of no appliance which fulfills so many different functions… Recently I remarked to friend that if I had to choose just one household appliance, it would be the electric skillet." Alas, the electric skillet is virtually extinct today, its utility diminished by more versatile electric ovens and stovetops.

New culinary tools also made their way into advertisements and cookbooks. "Make this Pineapple Upside-Down Cake with your Favorite Cake Mix…and turn it out perfect in Reynolds Wrap, The Pure Aluminum Foil!" declared a Reynolds print ad from the 1950s. Roberta Ames gave a nod to Reynolds Wrap (or perhaps it was an early example of product placement) in her pineapple upside-down cake recipe when she wrote, "The Reynolds Home Economic Staff suggested the use of foil in upside-down cake. This method does beautifully, and the cake is easier to remove than if baked right in the pan." It does indeed work beautifully, and this adaptation of Ames' pineapple upside-down cake includes this helpful tip. From the looks of Kitty's version, she kept Reynolds Wrap on hand, too.

Pineapple Upside-Down Cake

ADAPTED FROM THE COMPLETE ELECTRIC SKILLET-FRYPAN
COOKBOOK *BY ROBERTA AMES (HEARTHSIDE PRESS, 1960)*

NOTE: We have adapted this recipe for a cast-iron skillet.

For the topping

> 5 *tablespoons butter*
>
> ¾ *cup brown sugar*
>
> 7–8 *canned pineapple slices (reserve syrup)*
>
> *Pecan halves, for decorating*
>
> *Maraschino cherries, for decorating*

For the cake

> 10 *tablespoons butter*
>
> 1½ *cups granulated sugar*
>
> 2 *large eggs*
>
> 2 *cups all-purpose flour*
>
> 3 *teaspoons baking powder*
>
> 1 *teaspoon salt*
>
> ½ *cup buttermilk*
>
> ¼ *cup syrup from pineapple can*
>
> 1 *teaspoon vanilla extract*

1. Line a 10-inch cast-iron skillet with aluminum foil, completely covering the bottom and sides and extending extra foil over edges of the pan. Preheat oven to 350°F.

2. Make the topping: Place butter in skillet, place skillet in oven, and melt butter. As soon as butter is melted, remove and stir in brown sugar, carefully mixing well with a rubber spatula so as not to tear foil. Arrange pineapple slices over

butter/sugar spread. Place cherries in center of pineapple and pecans between the slices.

3. Make the batter: In the bowl of an electric mixer, cream butter, adding sugar gradually, and then add eggs and beat well. Stir flour, baking powder, and salt together in a small bowl. Combine buttermilk, syrup, and vanilla in a small measuring cup. Add flour mixture alternately with buttermilk/syrup mixture, beating well after each addition. Spread batter evenly across mixture in skillet.

4. Bake for approximately 45–50 minutes, or until toothpick inserted in center of cake comes out clean. Place a large cake plate over pan, and invert to remove. Peel off aluminum foil, pressing back any pineapple that may be stuck to the foil.

YIELD: 10–12 SERVINGS

See color insert.

Some months after delivering the baby she conceived with Pete Campbell, Peggy Olson makes plans to have dinner with her mother, Katherine, and her sister, Anita Olson Respola, at their Brooklyn home. Peggy arrives late from work in Manhattan, and walks in carrying a vacuum cleaner she's borrowed. Katherine and Anita have already eaten and are sitting in the kitchen.

Katherine, an old-school, devout Catholic mother, fears for Peggy's soul. She urges Peggy to attend church, telling her that her late father would like it if she lit a candle for him. As Katherine leaves the room, she tells Peggy, "I pray for you."

"She's not going to be here forever," says Anita. "Would it kill you to go?"

Peggy, who is increasingly asserting her independence and breaking away from her cloistered Brooklyn upbringing for a career in Manhattan, replies, "I don't want to and I'm capable of making my own decisions."

In response, Anita, whose shame and anger over her younger sister's baby will soon bubble over in a church confession (season 2, episode 4; "Three Sundays") delivers one of the most damning lines spoken in *Mad Men*: "Really? The State of New York didn't think so. The doctors didn't think so."

Even the heavenly looking coffee cake on Katherine's kitchen table couldn't take the sting out of that.

The notion of a sweet cake taken with coffee originated in Europe in the seventeenth century. Sweet yeast breads were common in north central Europe and, when coffee was introduced in the 1600s, people discovered the two went well together. As the Germans and Dutch began arriving in New York, New Jersey, and Delaware, they brought their recipes for breads and cakes with them. "All of these colonial cooks made fruity, buttery breakfast or coffee cakes from recipes that vary only slightly from methods used in the twentieth century," according to Evan Jones, author of *American Food: The Gastronomic Story* (Vintage Books, 1981). Even so, the term *coffee cake* itself was first used centuries later in the 1870s.

There are countless coffee cake variations, and we tested several before deciding that Katherine Olson's coffee cake likely would have been, as most coffee cakes of the 1960s were, buttery, with more than a hint of cinnamon and a slight crunch on top. We found a recipe we believe Katherine would have liked—with a layer of meringue and jelly—in *What Cooks in Suburbia* by Lila Perl (1961). This treat might even be sweet enough to temper Anita's bitterness.

"She may dwell...in an urban apartment building, a semi-urban garden apartment, or on a more spacious acreage of her own in a fashionable exurb," wrote Perl in dedicating her book to the Modern Suburban Homemaker, "but if she has a kitchen, a family, and an entourage, large or small, of friends and neighbors, she is—for the purposes of this book—a suburban homemaker." She's talking to you, Katherine.

Sour Cream Coffee Cake

FROM WHAT COOKS IN SUBURBIA *BY LILA PERL (E.P. DUTTON & CO., 1961)*

NOTE: To make a coffee cake ring you can bake this cake in a 9-cup Bundt pan. Place half of the topping in the greased pan, followed by half of the batter, the remainder of the topping, the meringue filling, and the remaining half of the batter. Cool cake slightly and turn onto plate. Author Lila Perl suggests serving this cake freshly baked, slightly warm from the oven "for extra-special acclaim."

For the brown sugar filling and topping

4 tablespoons brown sugar

2 tablespoons rolled oats

½ teaspoon ground cinnamon

2 tablespoons butter

2 tablespoons chopped walnuts

For the meringue filling

1 egg white, at room temperature

⅓ cup tart jam or jelly

For the batter

1⅔ cups sifted all-purpose flour

1 teaspoon baking powder

1 teaspoon baking soda

½ teaspoon salt

4 tablespoons butter

4 tablespoons vegetable shortening

1 cup granulated sugar

2 large eggs

1 cup sour cream

1 teaspoon vanilla extract

1. Butter an 8 x 8 x 2-inch baking pan. Preheat oven to 350°F.

2. Make the brown sugar filling and topping: In a small bowl, combine the brown sugar, rolled oats, and cinnamon. Cut in the butter until the mixture is crumbly. Add the nuts and set aside.

3. Make the meringue filling: Beat egg white until very stiff. Beat in the jam or jelly a tablespoon at a time. Set aside.

4. Make the batter: In a medium bowl, sift together flour, baking powder, baking soda, and salt. In a large bowl, cream the butter, shortening, and sugar. Add the eggs one at a time, beat well, and blend in the sour cream and vanilla. Add flour mixture and beat just until lumps disappear.

5. Spoon half of the batter into the pan. Spread batter until smooth and sprinkle with half of the brown sugar filling. Place the jam or jelly meringue on top of the filling by spoonfuls, distributing in equal quantities over the surface. Do not smooth meringue.

6. Spoon remaining batter over meringue, distributing it evenly. Sprinkle the remaining half of the brown sugar topping on top of the batter and bake for 55 minutes, or until cake springs back to touch. Cool slightly and cut into squares.

YIELD: 1 8-INCH CAKE

HENRY AND BETTY'S APRICOT APPLE PIE

SEASON 3, EPISODE 7
"Seven Twenty Three"

One afternoon, not long after Betty Draper gives birth to her and Don's third child, she hosts a tea for a few members of the Tarrytown Junior League who are trying to stop construction of a water tank in Ossining that will drain the Pleasantville Road Reservoir. When it's suggested they need help from the governor's office, Betty calls Henry Francis, the man she met at Jane and Roger Sterling's garden party (season 3, episode 3; "My Old Kentucky Home") who works as an

NEW YORK GOVERNOR NELSON ROCKEFELLER AND HIS NEW BRIDE, MARGARETTA LARGE FITLER MURPHY, BETTER KNOWN AS "HAPPY," IN 1963

aide to New York governor Nelson Rockefeller. In fact, Henry went to Roger's party directly from Rockefeller's wedding to a woman named Happy. Conveniently, Henry says he's driving upstate the next morning and suggests they have a cup of coffee at Swenson's Bakery in Ossining, followed by a hike to the reservoir.

At Swenson's, Henry orders apple pie for them both and asks Betty if she prefers ice cream or cheddar cheese.

"One of each," Betty replies.

Contrary to the expression, "as American as apple pie," this popular dessert existed long before Thomas Jefferson penned the Declaration of Independence. It's been around since at least the late fourteenth century (if you count the apple tart). The idea of topping apple pie with ice cream dates to the 1890s, but it's harder to pin down the origins of pairing apple pie with cheese (typically a sharp cheddar). Some say the practice originated in England and was popularized in New England, but even apple pie authority John T. Edge, the author of *Apple Pie: An American Story* (G.P. Putnam's Sons, 2004), threw up his hands trying to ascertain its origins. Most apple varieties, at least until the mid-1800s, were tart, not sweet, and sharp cheese blended well with the tartness of the apples. Major cheese manufacturers such as Kraft and Borden promoted a slice of cheese as a complement to apple pie in the mid-twentieth century, but the practice has since gone out of favor.

To mark what one might call Henry and Betty's "first date," an apple pie with a Rockefeller connection seems called for; after all, that's what Betty was looking for to help save her reservoir—a Rockefeller connection. In 1965, Happy Rockefeller contributed a recipe for glazed New York state apples—that also calls for apricots—to *The Congressional Club Cook Book* (Congressional Club, 1965), which featured recipes from members of Congress, governors, and the diplomatic corps and their spouses. We turned Happy's recipe into a pie.

For guidance, and the pie pastry, we used a Pillsbury Bake-Off–winning recipe for apple date pie from *Best of the Bake-Off Collection* by Ann Pillsbury (1959). The Pillsbury Bake-Off competition began in 1949 (it was called the "Grand National Recipe and Baking Contest" back then) and offered $100,000 in prizes to housewives, including $50,000 to the first-place winner, willing to put their baking recipes to the test at the Waldorf-Astoria Hotel.

Apricot apple pie is easy enough to top with ice cream or cheese, but if you prefer cheese, we suggest a topping from *The New Can Opener Cookbook* (Crowell, 1959) by Poppy Cannon, one of many period cookbooks built around a new appliance of convenience. "At one time a badge of shame, hallmark of the lazy lady and careless wife," wrote Cannon, "today the can opener is fast becoming a magic wand."

Given Henry's association with Nelson Rockefeller, we think he'd enjoy an apple pie inspired by the governor's wife. As for Betty, we always had the sense she'd like to bake her own apple pie and eat it, too.

Apricot Apple Pie

FILLING ADAPTED FROM RECIPE FOR GLAZED NEW YORK STATE APPLES FROM MRS. NELSON A. ROCKEFELLER, WIFE OF THE GOVERNOR OF NEW YORK, IN THE CONGRESSIONAL CLUB COOK BOOK (CONGRESSIONAL CLUB, 1965);

CRUST RECIPE ADAPTED FROM PILLSBURY'S BEST OF THE BAKE-OFF COLLECTION (CONSOLIDATED BOOK PUBLISHERS, 1959);

CHEESE TOPPING INSTRUCTIONS ADAPTED FROM THE NEW CAN OPENER COOKBOOK BY POPPY CANNON (CROWELL, 1959)

NOTE: Mrs. Rockefeller's recipe called for New York state apples. We prefer a mix of New York Empires and Granny Smith apples. However, use the combination of apples you prefer for baking.

If using fresh apricots, use 4 tablespoons of flour.

For the piecrust (recipe for a double-crust pie)

3 cups all–purpose flour

¼ teaspoon salt

1 tablespoon sugar

1 cup butter or vegetable shortening

8–12 tablespoons ice water

For the filling

½ cup dried apricots cut into small pieces, or 4 fresh apricots, also cut into small pieces (see note above)

5–6 cups apples, peeled, cored, and sliced (see note above)

3–4 tablespoons all-purpose flour (see note above)

1 cup sugar

¾ teaspoon ground cinnamon

¼ teaspoon ground nutmeg

2 teaspoons fresh lemon juice

1 tablespoon butter

1. Make the piecrust: Sift the flour, salt, and sugar together in a medium bowl. Cut in the butter or shortening using a pastry cutter or a fork until mixture is the size of small peas. Sprinkle ice water over mixture while lightly mixing with a fork until the dough is just moist enough to hold together. Divide the dough in half.

2. Form the dough into two balls, and then into two flat disks ½ inch thick. Cover with plastic wrap and refrigerate for at least 30 minutes or until ready to use.

3. Lightly flour a rolling surface. With a lightly floured rolling pin, roll a ball of dough out into a circle 1½ inches larger than your pie plate. Lift the dough from the rolling surface and place in pie plate. Gently press crust flat against the bottom and sides. Trim off excess.

4. Make the filling: If using dried apricots, place apricots in a small saucepan, cover with water, and cook over medium heat until soft, about 15 minutes. Remove from heat.

5. In a large bowl, toss apples with apricots, flour, sugar, cinnamon, nutmeg, and lemon juice. Spoon mixture into prepared dough, leaving extra liquid in the bowl. Dot with butter.

6. Roll remaining dough and gently lay over filling, trim off excess, and crimp edge to finish. Cut small slits in the top crust in two or three places.

7. Bake at 425°F for 15 minutes. Lower temperature to 375°F and bake for 40–45 minutes, or until pie is lightly golden brown.

To top your pie with melted cheese:

> *2 tablespoons melted butter*
> *Cheddar cheese (can be prepackaged slices)*
> *sliced into inch-wide strips*
> *Grated nutmeg*

1. Preheat oven to 350°F. Brush the top of the pie lightly with melted butter.

2. Arrange cheese slices on top of the pie like spokes of a wheel or in a lattice pattern. Sprinkle lightly with grated nutmeg and set in oven for 10 minutes or until cheese has melted. When serving, the pie should be brought warm to the table.

FAYE MILLER'S CHOCOLATE CHIP COOKIES

SEASON 4, EPISODE 2

"Christmas Comes But Once a Year"

Dr. Faye Miller is something of a commercial anthropologist. She and her firm, the Motivational Research Group, use focus groups and reams of demographic data to divine the way consumers think and to help devise pathways to their wallets. We first meet Faye when Bert Cooper arranges a presentation for the senior staff of Sterling Cooper Draper Pryce so they can learn about her firm's services.

Faye hands out a questionnaire as she begins her presentation for those present to complete, a way of familiarizing them with her research methods, and points to a jar of chocolate chip cookies she's placed on the conference room table.

"Please, take a cookie," she says cheerfully.

Concerned that his every move is now under scrutiny for what it reveals about him, Harry Crane asks, "What's it mean if we don't?"

"That you're a psychopath," she replies in jest. "The point of the cookies," she adds as Harry reaches into the jar, "is that everyone should be rewarded for their time."

The questions, she goes on to explain, have been designed to determine what consumers *really* want as opposed to what they say they want; to get to the real feelings below the surface. When she points out that one of the questions is "How would you describe your father?"—a question that hits at one of the most painful parts of Don Draper's life—we know it's only a matter of time before he excuses himself from the exercise. Don has little use for Faye's analytical social science approach; he operates on instinct, intuition, and insight. Though Don is skeptical of her methods, Don and Faye will, inevitably, succumb to a mutual but ill-fated attraction.

In season 4, episode 4 ("The Rejected"), when Faye organizes a focus group comprising the young, single women who work at Sterling Cooper Draper Pryce on behalf of client Pond's Cold Cream, the reward is Danish pastries. But we prefer sumptuous, fresh-baked chocolate chip cookies, and would happily fill out Faye's questionnaire for one.

This chocolate chip cookie recipe is from *Better Homes and Gardens Cookies and Candies* (1966) because it seems to capture the most salient point here: "Happiness," says *Better Homes and Gardens*, "is a warm cookie."

Chocolate Chip Cookies

FROM BETTER HOMES AND GARDENS
COOKIES AND CANDIES *(MEREDITH, 1966)*

1 cup all-purpose flour

½ teaspoon baking soda

½ teaspoon salt

½ cup (1 stick) butter, softened

½ cup granulated sugar

¼ cup light brown sugar, packed

1 large egg

½ teaspoon vanilla extract

6 ounces (1 cup) semisweet chocolate morsels

½ cup chopped walnuts

1. Preheat oven to 375°F. Sift flour, baking soda, and salt together in a small bowl. In the bowl of a mixer, cream butter, both sugars, egg, and vanilla until fluffy.

2. Stir dry ingredients into mixture. Stir in morsels and nuts. Drop by rounded teaspoonfuls 2 inches apart onto greased baking sheets. Bake for 10–12 minutes, or until golden brown. Remove from oven and cool slightly. Remove from baking sheet.

YIELD: 36 COOKIES

POPCORN BALLS

SEASON 4, EPISODE 2

"Christmas Comes But Once a Year"

During the festivities at the Sterling Cooper Draper Pryce Christmas party in 1964 (see Canadian Clubhouse Punch and Lucky Strike Holiday Eggnog, page 54), a conga line forms and snakes through the office, past tables laden with holiday treats. We spotted a classic next to the candy canes: a bowl of red and white popcorn balls.

There are accounts, perhaps apocryphal, that Native Americans gave English settlers in Massachusetts popcorn balls made with maple syrup at the first Thanksgiving. It is at least fair to say that popcorn balls bound with syrup or molasses have been around for well over a century, according to Andrew F. Smith, author of *Popped Culture: A Social History of Popcorn in America* (Smithsonian, 2001). Popcorn's various forms, including popcorn threaded onto lengths of string, have been a part of festive decorations for Christmas and other holidays at least since the late nineteenth century. In the 1960s, popcorn balls were popular Halloween treats and sold at country fairs, ball games, and the circus.

Popcorn ball recipes proliferated in the United States after the Civil War. The techniques and ingredients varied, but the basic concept was the same: use a heated adhering agent—syrup, sugar, or molasses—then add salt and butter and use the agent to shape the popcorn into a sphere. Flavorings such as chocolate, peppermint and vanilla were eventually added, as were foods like strawberries, nuts, and marshmallows to embellish the original. Additives such as food coloring could turn a normally white popcorn ball into an edible Christmas decoration, like the red and white popcorn balls on display at the Sterling Cooper Christmas party.

This recipe for popcorn balls is derived from *Betty Crocker's New Boys and Girls Cookbook* (1965), but this recipe uses marshmallows and butter in place of molasses to hold the popcorn together.

At the insistence of Lee Garner, Jr., the firm's most important client, Roger Sterling dons a Santa suit at the holiday party. He looks pretty forlorn wearing it, but maybe a popcorn ball will restore his Christmas cheer. That and a few martinis.

Popcorn Balls

ADAPTED FROM BETTY CROCKER'S NEW BOYS AND GIRLS COOKBOOK

(GOLDEN PRESS—WESTERN PUBLISHING COMPANY, INC., 1965)

7 cups freshly popped popcorn

3 cups mini marshmallows

2 tablespoons butter

¼ teaspoon salt

1. Place popcorn in large buttered bowl. Heat marshmallows, butter, and salt in the top of a double boiler, or in the microwave, until melted.

2. Pour marshmallow mixture over popcorn and stir gently to coat. Grease hands with butter and quickly shape popcorn into 2-inch balls. Wrap in waxed paper.

YIELD: APPROXIMATELY 12 2-INCH BALLS

BARBETTA'S PEARS BAKED IN RED WINE ALLA PIEMONTESE

SEASON 4, EPISODE 8

"The Summer Man"

Barbetta, the elegant Piemontese restaurant where Don Draper and his beautiful date Bethany Van Nuys dine (see Barbetta's Roasted Fresh Peppers alla Bagna Cauda, page 125), generously shared a dessert recipe with us as well. Pears baked in red wine alla Piemontese, like their roasted fresh peppers alla bagna cauda, first appeared on Barbetta's menu in 1962, and would have been the perfect way for Don and Bethany to keep the warmth of the evening going.

Pears Baked in Red Wine alla Piemontese

COURTESY OF BARBETTA RESTAURANT, NEW YORK, NEW YORK

6 ripe Bosc pears

2 cups red wine

¼ cup sugar

6 cloves

1 cinnamon stick

¼ cup lemon juice

1. Preheat oven to 300°F. Wash and dry pears. Place pears in a baking pan that accommodates 6 pears (lay them flat). In a small bowl, pour the red wine and add sugar, cloves, cinnamon stick, and lemon juice. Stir until sugar dissolves. Pour mixture into the baking pan and place in oven. Turn pears after 5 minutes and brush with liquid in pan.

2. Bake for approximately 1 hour (cooking time may vary depending on size and ripeness of pears), continuing to brush the pears every 10 minutes. Pears should be slightly crinkly. Remove pan from oven and allow to cool to room temperature. Serve with extra red wine sauce.

YIELD: 6 SERVINGS

See color insert.

LINDY'S CHERRY CHEESECAKE
SEASON 4, EPISODE 9
"The Beautiful Girls"

When Roger Sterling and Joan Harris return to the Tip Toe Inn, a Jewish deli on the corner of Broadway and 86th Street they frequented during their affair, Joan asks Roger why they always went there.

"No chance of running in to anyone and, of course, the cherry cheesecake," replies Roger as he slides a forkful into his mouth.

The Tip Toe Inn is long gone, but for decades it was known for its corned beef and pastrami sandwiches, smoked sturgeon, lox, gefilte fish, borscht, and its cheesecake. Details of the Tip Toe Inn's cherry cheesecake recipe are not known, so we turned to Lindy's, the New York deli with the most famous cheesecake at the time. The recipe was long sought by food writers, cookbook authors, and patrons.

Lindy's was "fabled for its sturgeon, corned beef, and blintzes," wrote the *New York Times'* Craig Claiborne in 1977. "But most of all it was renowned for its cheesecakes which were as integral a part of Gotham culture as Yankee Stadium, Coney Island, Grant's Tomb, and the Staten Island Ferry."

According to William Grimes' 2009 book *Appetite City: A Culinary History of New York*, Lindy's was "the archetypal show-business canteen...[t]he food and the atmosphere were casual, and Jewish. The waiters bickered with the customers, who bickered back, pretended to be annoyed, and loved every minute of it. Actors and comedians drifted from table to table, greeting friends and trading wisecracks."

Harpo Marx, who usually had little to say in the movies, called Lindy's cheesecake "ambrosia," and the cheesecake itself became something of a Broadway star. In the hit show *Guys and Dolls,* based on several short stories by Damon Runyon, Lindy's became Mindy's, and the question of whether Mindy's sells more strudel or cheesecake was the subject of a bet between gamblers Nathan Detroit and Sky Masterson.

Cheesecake is the ultimate indulgence, rich yet somehow light, smooth, creamy, and irresistible. As Roger correctly points out, cheesecake was served "to the Olympic athletes in ancient Greece," (season 1, episode 7; "Red in the Face"), though we imagine it must have been the victor's just deserts because cheesecake eaten before a competition could only slow an athlete down.

Numerous magazines and cookbooks purported to have Lindy's original recipe, and many variants appeared in print. In her book *How America Eats* (1960), the legendary Clementine Paddleford, a food writer for the *New York Herald Tribune* and food editor for *This Week* Magazine (see Palm Springs Chile Rellenos, page 98), claimed that Leo Lindemann, Lindy himself, gave the recipe to her. One of Lindy cheesecake's most distinctive features was the "cookie dough crust," unlike the graham cracker crust we find in today's cheesecake recipes.

Serve it with the cherry topping Roger loved so much, and you'll add a pound sterling to the waist of every dinner guest. But, don't worry; they can work it off at the next Olympics.

Lindy's Cherry Cheesecake

ADAPTED FROM HOW AMERICA EATS BY CLEMENTINE PADDLEFORD (SCRIBNER, 1960)

For the cookie crust

> 1 *cup sifted all-purpose flour*
>
> ¼ *cup sugar*
>
> 1 *teaspoon grated lemon peel*
>
> *Pinch of vanilla bean (inside pulp) or*
>> ¼ *teaspoon vanilla extract*
>
> 1 *egg yolk*
>
> ½ *cup butter*

For the cheese filling

> 2½ *pounds cream cheese*
>
> 1¾ *cups sugar*
>
> 3 *tablespoons all-purpose flour*
>
> 1½ *teaspoons grated orange peel*
>
> 1½ *teaspoons grated lemon peel*
>
> *Pinch of vanilla bean (inside pulp) or*
>> ¼ *teaspoon vanilla extract*
>
> 5 *eggs, plus 2 egg yolks*
>
> ¼ *cup heavy cream*

For the topping

> 1 *21-ounce can cherry pie filling*

1. Make the crust: Combine flour, sugar, lemon peel, and vanilla. Make a well in the center and add egg yolk and butter. Work together quickly with hands until well blended. Wrap in waxed paper and chill thoroughly in refrigerator, about an hour.

2. Make the cheese filling: In the large bowl of a mixer, combine

cream cheese, sugar, flour, orange and lemon peel, and vanilla. Add whole eggs and egg yolks, one at a time, stirring lightly after each addition. Stir in cream.

3. Remove dough from refrigerator. Divide dough in half. Roll one half on a floured board until ⅛ inch thick. Place over oiled or buttered bottom of 9-inch springform cake pan. Trim excess dough. Reassemble pan and butter or oil sides. Bake at 400°F for 20 minutes, or until a light golden color. Cool. Increase oven temperature to 475°F.

4. Butter or oil interior sides of cake form and place over base. Press remaining dough against sides of pan. Fill form with cheese mixture and bake at 475°F for 12–15 minutes. Reduce temperature to 200°F and continue baking for 1 hour. Let the cake cool for at least 2 hours.

5. When cool, spoon cherry pie filling over top of cake. Cover and refrigerate for several hours before serving. Remove from refrigerator at least 30 minutes before serving.

YIELD: 12–16 SERVINGS

SALLY'S FRENCH TOAST (WITH RUM)

SEASON 4, EPISODE 9

"The Beautiful Girls"

Don and Betty Draper's divorce takes a big toll on daughter Sally, who's now on the cusp of adolescence, and she begins acting out. She's brought home from a sleepover in the middle of the night by a friend's mother who caught her "touching herself." Much to Betty's disapproval, she continues to meet the neighborhood boy, Glen Bishop, at an abandoned lot near their homes. She is moody and prone to outbursts of anger. Thanks to a kindly therapist, Sally eventually begins to better manage her anger and confusion.

While spending a night with Don in his drab Greenwich Village apartment, Sally announces she wants to live with him all the time. Don is awakened the next morning by the sounds of Sally at work in the kitchen. As he enters the living area he sees Sally emerging from the kitchen, proudly holding two plates.

"I made French toast," she says confidently, "and there's no shells in it." When she suggests they watch *The Today Show* while they eat, it is apparent that Don's little girl is starting to become a young woman.

As Don downs his first bite, a look of puzzlement crosses his face. Sally has mistaken a bottle of rum for Mrs. Butterworth's syrup.

"Is that bad?" asks Sally.

"Not really," says Don taking another bite, pleasantly surprised by the serendipitous recipe Sally has created.

Sally's French Toast (with Rum) is based on a French toast recipe that appeared in *1001 Dairy Dishes from the Sealtest Kitchens* by the National Dairy Products Corporation (1963), a company that happened to be located on Madison Avenue in New York, not far from the offices of Sterling Cooper. An individual recipe or a cookbook was a popular marketing tool in the 1960s; many companies, such as Sealtest, French's, Bacardi, and others encouraged readers to write in for recipes or cookbooks that promoted the use of their products.

"Milk has been food and drink to mankind, a unique staple item in his diet, long before recorded history," reads the grandiloquent preface to *1001 Dairy Dishes from the Sealtest Kitchens*. It declares milk a *sine qua non* of civilization itself, which, it says, "became possible only after the cow and other milk-giving animals were domesticated and primitive agriculture began some eleven thousand years ago." Be that as it may, we know there are some, perhaps even Don, who would make the same claim for rum.

French Toast (with Rum)

FRENCH TOAST ADAPTED FROM 1001 DAIRY DISHES FROM THE SEALTEST KITCHENS
(NATIONAL DAIRY PRODUCTS CORPORATION, 1963)

2 eggs

1 cup milk

¼ teaspoon ground cinnamon

1 tablespoon rum

1 teaspoon maple syrup

6 slices bread

Butter, for frying

1. Beat eggs slightly. Stir in milk, cinnamon, rum, and syrup. Pour into shallow, flat dish.

2. Dip each slice of bread into mixture, turning it, and allowing time for both sides to soak up liquid. Fry slowly in butter on both sides. Serve immediately with butter and maple syrup.

YIELD: 6 SLICES

WHEN IN NEW YORK...

A Handy List of *Mad Men* Haunts

Many of the bars and restaurants frequented by Don Draper, Roger Sterling, and other *Mad Men* characters are still alive and well in New York City; several contributed recipes for this book. If you're planning a trip to the Big Apple, you may want to visit them. Tell them Bert Cooper sent you.

ALGONQUIN HOTEL
59 West 44th Street
(212) 840-6800

Home to the Round Table, a favorite of New York's busness and creative elite (see page 24)

BARBETTA
321 West 46th Street
(212) 246-9171

Authentic cuisine from Italy's Piedmont region served amidst rare antiques in a refined atmosphere in the Theater District (see page 125)

THE DUBLIN HOUSE
225 West 79th Street
(212) 874-9528

An authentic Irish Pub on the Upper West Side (see page 52)

GRAND CENTRAL OYSTER BAR
89 East 42nd Street
212 490-6650

The city's most famous oyster bar, located in one of New York's architectural gems, Grand Central Station (see page 82)

KEENS STEAKHOUSE
73 West 36th Street
(212) 947-3636

Rich in tradition and atmosphere, as well as sumptuous steaks (don't forget the Caesar) (see page 144)

THE OAK BAR
10 Central Park South
(212) 758-7777

An elegant, romantic, richly appointed bar in the Plaza Hotel
(see page 65)

THE PALM
837 Second Avenue
(212) 687-2953

A seafood restaurant/steakhouse with an Italian twist (see page 137)

P.J. CLARKE'S
915 Third Avenue
(212) 317-1616 and

A New York institution serving hearty fare and drink (see page 20)

THE PIERRE HOTEL
2 East 61st Street
(212) 838-8000

Featuring the Two E Bar/Lounge, the modern incarnation of The
Pierre's famed Tea Room (see page 18)

THE ROOSEVELT HOTEL
45 East 45th Street
(212) 661-9600

Known as the Grand Dame of Madison Avenue, offering many dining
and drinking options

SARDI'S
234 West 44th Street
(212) 221-8440

The culinary heart of Broadway, with walls lined with caricatures of
Broadway's leading lights (see page 89)

THE WALDORF-ASTORIA HOTEL
301 Park Avenue
(212) 872-1275 (restaurant reservation line)

The legendary hotel once owned by Conrad Hilton, with a kitchen so famous they named a salad after it (see page 150)

THE ROOSEVELT IS THE SETTING FOR MANY *MAD MEN* SCENES. IN SEASON 1 IT'S WHERE SAL HAS TO CONFRONT HIS REPRESSED HOMOSEXUALITY WHEN, OVER DINNER, THE MAN FROM BELLE JOLIE LIPSTICK EXPRESSES HIS ROMANTIC INTEREST. AND IT'S WHERE DON TAKES UP TEMPORARY RESIDENCE IN SEASON 2 WHEN HIS MARRIAGE TO BETTY HITS A LOW.

THANK YOU NOTES

Cooking up a book like this requires the efforts of many people whose names don't end up on the cover, and we'd like to thank each and every one of them.

First, you need an agent you really like, and not just because she flatters you by liking your ideas. Like Joan Holloway, a good agent knows who will play nicely together. She makes the match between the author(s) and the publisher. So, thanks to Joelle Delbourgo for bringing everyone to the table.

When you work with an editor for the first time, it's a bit like Don Draper's blind date with Bethany Van Nuys. You're hoping for the best and so are they. We don't know if our editor, Leah Wilson, would come to dinner again, but we'd call *her* any time we needed a creative, smart, enthusiastic, and talented editor.

Glenn Yeffeth is the Bert Cooper of this production. He's the head honcho at BenBella Books, our publisher, and is ultimately responsible for the final product. We're curious to know if he sits at a big desk and eats chocolate pudding out of a parfait glass. We all owe our thanks to Glenn because he's picking up the tab for this party.

At any good dinner party, you need someone to set the table, make the flower arrangements, and ensure that what you're serving up looks classy, even if there were a few disasters in the kitchen. At Sterling Cooper that job belongs to art director Salvatore Romano. Our version of Sal is Faceout Studio, the people who designed this book. Just as a beautiful table enhances a well-prepared meal, a terrific design adds life to words on the page.

When you're cooking for a large group you need help in the kitchen. After all, Don Draper didn't do it all by himself. He may have been an ad man par excellence, but without the account men, secretaries, copywriters, and artists his ideas were, well, just ideas. We consulted with the proprietors, chefs, bartenders, and managers of many of the hotels, restaurants, and brands featured in this book, as well as a small army of volunteer recipe testers and tasters who ensured that the recipes in this book were actually palatable on the plate.

We are especially grateful to Alex Aubry and Rodney Landers of the Algonquin Hotel; Joseph Calle of Angelo's of Mulberry Street; Patricia Suau and Joe Gerbino of Bacardi; Laura Maioglio of Barbetta; Robert Rouleau and Wendy Schnee of the Beverly Hills Hotel; Mimi Jonas of Canadian Club; Paula Griffin of the Dublin House; Sue Lappi and Susan Wakefield of General Mills; Sandy Ingber and Jonathan Young of the Grand Central Oyster Bar; Ashley Henry and Charity Lifka of Hormel Foods; Bill Rodgers of Keens Steakhouse; Vivian Santangelo of Meredith Corporation; Laurie Austin of the John F. Kennedy Memorial Library; Priscilla Fujimura of the Oak Bar; Ryan Drushel of the Taj Pierre Hotel; Peter Seely and Kristen Lawrence of Trader Vic's; Jade Moore, Phil Pratt, and Tara Wright of the '21' Club; Kate Strotman of the Palm Restaurant; Doug Quinn, Paul Tumpowsky, Thea Scotti, and Jackie Singer of P.J. Clarke's; Joy Percival; Steve and Christian Rockefeller; Michele Hiltzik of the Rockefeller Archive Center and Happy Rockefeller for permission to use a photo of her wedding day; Alison Cory of the Roosevelt Hotel; Ken Biberaj of the Russian Tea Room; Max Klimavicius of Sardi's; Marcie Rudell of Stork Club Enterprises; Alec Sivel and Joann Miller of Utz Quality Foods; and Jonathan Stas of the Waldorf-Astoria Hotel.

Our hard-working, opinionated recipe testers and tasters were indispensible: Linda Bauer, Sue Bonaiuto, Andi Brown, Heidi Brown, Laurie Burgess, Suzanne Church, Sharon Conway, Joan Demers, Mary Kate Dillon, Denise Dirocco, Kim Evans, Jody Feinberg, Andy Gelman, Doris Gelman (who also took on the task of proofreading recipes), Lois Gelman (who made invaluable comments on the entire manuscript), Anne Marie Gluck, Roma Hoyt, Eileen O'Keefe, Bill and Debbie Pryor, Jayne Raphael, Judy Safian, Daniela Sever, Donna Skinner (who also spent hours helping prepare *Mad Men*–themed cocktail and dinner parties), Diana Zais, Cathy Zheutlin, Leslie Zheutlin, and Barbara Zheutlin. No cookbook worth its salt could be written without honest feedback and repeated testing, retesting, and fine-tuning of recipes. Our friends and families are the unsung heroes of the book you hold in your hands.

Presentation is also very important where food is concerned. Photographer Nina Gallant and food stylist Catrine Kelty are responsible for many of the mouth-watering images in this book, and we are grateful for both their enthusiasm for this project and their artistry.

And last, but not least, if you have a party like this you want to be sure the gossip columnists, the wags, and the paparazzi know about it. You need a great pitchman like Jimmy "There's no nuts in Utz" Barrett. Jennifer Canzoneri and Heather Butterfield at BenBella were our Jimmy Barrett, just much less offensive.

In addition we thank Vicki Krupp, Judy's co-author on three previous books, who was a great sounding board for ideas and was generous—and spot-on—with her advice. Thanks, too, to Robert Hess, co-founder of the Museum of the American Cocktail in New Orleans, who is an extraordinary font of information about cocktail history. We are grateful to Diana Carey of the Schlesinger Library at Radcliffe College and the librarians of the Needham, Massachusetts, Public Library for their assistance.

Judy would like to thank her gifted yoga teachers at STIL Studio—Kevan Gale, Betty Riaz, Lauren Koenig-Plonskier, and Allison Lessner Newman—for providing many moments of peace.

So, our thanks to each and every one.

IMAGE CREDITS

Main Text

Pages 10, 12, and 56: Photos and image courtesy of Canadian Club

Pages 15, 17, and 92: Photos courtesy of Trader Vic's

Page 22: Photo courtesy of P.J. Clarke's

Page 24: Photo courtesy of the Algonquin Hotel

Pages 34 and 43: Photos courtesy of the '21' Club

Page 39: Photo courtesy of Stork Club Enterprises LLC

Pages 40 and 41: Photos courtesy of the Beverly Hills Hotel

Page 47: Image courtesy of Bacardi

Page 64: Photo courtesy of the Oak Bar

Page 68: Photo courtesy of Joy Percival

Page 80: Photo courtesy of Utz Quality Foods, Inc.

Page 83: Photo courtesy of the Grand Central Oyster Bar

Page 89: Photo courtesy of Sardi's

Page 110: Image courtesy of the General Mills Archives

Page 127: Photo courtesy of Barbetta

Page 133: Photo credit: Abbie Rowe, National Park Service/John F. Kennedy Presidential Library and Museum, Boston

Pages 144, 145, and 149: Photos courtesy of Keens Steakhouse

Page 150: Photo courtesy of the Waldorf-Astoria Hotel

Page 162: Photo credit: The Schlesinger Library, Radcliffe Institute, Harvard University

Page 171: Photo credit: Robert Knudsen, White House/John F. Kennedy Presidential Library and Museum, Boston

Page 195: Images courtesy of Hormel Foods; MARY KITCHEN® is a registered trademark of Hormel Foods, LLC, and is being used with permission from Hormel Foods Corporation

Page 202: Photo courtesy of the Russian Tea Room

Page 216: The Better Homes and Gardens New Cookbook © 1930 Meredith Corporation; Betty Crocker Hostess Cookbook cover image courtesy of the General Mills Archives

Page 225: Photo courtesy of the Rockefeller Archive Center

Page 245: Photo courtesy of the Roosevelt Hotel

Color Insert

"Martini" photo courtesy of the Algonquin Hotel

"Mint Julep" photo courtesy of the '21' Club

"Chicken Kiev" photo courtesy of the Russian Tea Room

All other photos: photography by Nina Gallant, food styling by Catrine Kelly

Section icons illustrated by Kritin Krantz

RECIPE INDEX

GENERAL INDEX

ABOUT THE AUTHORS

JUDY GELMAN is co-author of *The Book Club Cookbook: Recipes and Food for Thought from Your Book Club's Favorite Books and Authors* (Penguin, 2004), the first cookbook designed for book discussion groups. The second edition of *The Book Club Cookbook* will be published in 2012.

She is also co-author of *The Kids' Book Club Book: Reading Ideas, Activities, and Smart Tips for Organizing Terrific Kids' Book Clubs* (Penguin, 2007) and *Table of Contents: From Breakfast with Anita Diamant to Dessert with James Patterson—A Generous Helping of Recipes, Writings and Insights from Today's Bestselling Authors* (Adams, 2010). She is co-creator of bookclubcookbook.com and kidsbookclubbook.com. She speaks about cooking, food, and reading to book and food enthusiasts across the country.

PETER ZHEUTLIN is the author of *Around the World on Two Wheels: Annie Londonderry's Extraordinary Ride* (Citadel Press, 2007) and the co-author, with Thomas B. Graboys, MD, of *Life in the Balance: A Physician's Memoir of Life, Love and Loss with Parkinson's Disease and Dementia* (Union Square Press, 2008). He is also the co-author, with Robert P. Smith, of *Riches Among the Ruins: Adventures in the Dark Corners of the Global Economy* (Amacom, 2009). Mr. Zheutlin has written for *The Boston Globe, The Christian Science Monitor, The Los Angeles Times, The New England Quarterly*, and numerous other publications in the United States and abroad.

WANT MORE SMART POP?

WWW.SMARTPOPBOOKS.COM

» Read a new free essay online everyday

» Plus sign up for email updates, check out our upcoming titles, and more